Exercising Initiative

Exploring Innovation and the Innovation Process

Roger Henry Appeldorn

ISBN-13: 978-1530839940
ISBN-10: 1530839947

DEDICATION

To all the mentors, supporters, and champions
who shaped my life and my career,
especially

my mother and father,
Allen Opland,
Norm Albrecht,
Kent Bracewell,
Arthur Kotz,
Emil Grieshaber,
and my wife, Marilyn

ACKNOWLEDGEMENT

This book was originally produced for use in a course titled The Physics of Innovation at Hamline University in Saint Paul, Minnesota. This course was made possible by initiatives in the College of Liberal Arts that drive student development through education, leadership, and community involvement. It is funded by generous donations.

To make a gift to this program, visit www.hamline.edu/giving or call (800) 767-5585. Be sure to specify the donation recipient as the "Innovation Studies Program Fund" or the "Appeldorn Family Endowment Fund."

All gifts made to Hamline are tax deductible. Hamline's tax identification number is:
41-0693960

HAMLINE
UNIVERSITY

Contents

Topic

Exercising Initiative

1.0 Objective

3M (Minnesota Mining and Manufacturing) is internationally recognized as one of, if not the, premier technology and product development leader in the world. The strategy and culture that led to this leadership grew out of a business venture in the early 1900s to produce and market abrasive minerals to the emerging automotive market that almost failed. Through its struggles to keep the business alive, a unique corporate culture and philosophy was inspired by William L. McKnight, 3M's chairman of the board from 1944 to 1966, and was implemented by a number of individuals including Richard Drew (the inventor of Scotch Tape), Richard P. Carlton (3M's first vice president of Research and Development), and numerous 3M employees. These leaders recognized the extraordinary value of employee initiative and creative skills. McKnight's vision for the role of management was to ensure that this initiative and creativeness of its employees were encouraged, developed, rewarded, and sustained.

This 3M culture came to fruition in the early1950s. For example, between 1950 and 1974, 3M created a diverse new-to-the-world business every twelve to eighteen months, with most of them reaching division status within a few years. To reach division status at 3M, a new business had to achieve sustainable annual sales in the range of $300 to $500 million (in today's dollars). Few, if any, corporations have ever matched this performance.

The 3M culture of innovation is most frequently referred to as "3M Innovation." Unfortunately, the terms "innovating" and "innovation" have become overused, misused, and misunderstood to such an extent that these words have all but lost their meaning. 3M Innovation, however, is unique and may be best described as "The 3M Innovation Process."

3M Innovation is defined as *"New ideas plus action or implementation, which results in an improvement, gain, or profit."* The "innovation process" brings into play the variety of actions and implementations needed to achieve the desired improvement, gain, or profit. These actions and implementations include, for example, understanding and promoting innovation, understanding customer needs, quantifying the new opportunity, identifying needed support technologies or activities, promoting or selling the idea (internally and externally), organizing and managing for innovation, and developing financial models.

The objective of the Innovation Studies Program is to introduce to and educate undergraduate students about the innovation process principles, techniques, and best practices in preparation for their future innovative careers.

1.01 Purpose

The purpose of this book is to describe how the 3M Innovation process that gave employees the freedom to innovate, exercise their initiative, and pursue their own ideas worked and facilitated the creation of a new technology platform and a number of successful new businesses during my 3M employment from 1955 to 1996. Included are selected stories, accounts, and observations that reflect the prevailing innovation process and culture at 3M during this period.

2.00 Discovering Innovation and the Innovation Process

While attending Hamline University in 1955, I desperately needed a job to finance my education. One day in late May, as luck would have it, I discovered a notice posted on the Hamline bookstore bulletin board. The 3M Company was looking for a part-time summer employee. I skipped classes that day, called the phone number on the note, and arranged for an interview. When I arrived at the 3M headquarters, the employment manager, Burton Baker, apologized for having me drive all the way out there because the position had already been filled. But since I was there, he quickly arranged a couple of interviews for me anyway. The interviews were pleasant, and at the end of the day they all thanked me for coming to 3M and wished me success in finding a job.

When I returned to my room that afternoon, there was a message tacked on my door. All it said was, "3M called. You got the job!" They had found a position for me in the Abrasive Converting Department. I didn't know it at the time, but that one-day event put me on a career path that not only lasted forty-one years, it also shaped my life.

At the time, 3M was just another corporation like all the other corporations in the Twin Cities area. But I was very thankful for the job they gave me. I knew very little about 3M. I knew about Scotch tape, which was becoming a popular item, and 3M sandpaper. Five years earlier, my mother, father, and I had driven from Saint Paul to Winona, Minnesota, to visit my sister. We took Highway 61 south past the 3M Chemolite Plant near Hastings. As we drove by it my father remarked, "Now there is a company to invest in. It's going places!" My father was a state legislator at the time and had worked with 3M to help get their new light retroreflective product "Scotchlite" approved for its use on license plates. He was not only impressed with the Scotchlite product but with the 3M engineers and marketing people as well.

The 3M I walked into in 1955 was an incredibly friendly organization. It was like a family and the people working there were affectionately referred to as "3M'ers." Office doors were rarely closed and there was a great deal of transparency between management and employees at all levels.

My first job was as a special order expediter. Salespeople would need a custom product sample for a customer and it was my job to put all the pieces together and ship it to them within a day or two. On occasion I had only a few hours to complete the order.

While making my rounds through the factory one day, I got on the elevator. A somewhat stout individual in overalls, accompanied by a couple of coworkers I had recently become acquainted with, got in the elevator behind me. When the elevator stopped at my floor, the three were blocking the door. After waiting for a few moments, I asked them to step aside because I had work to do. The stout gentleman laughed, stepped aside, and let me pass.

Later, one of the coworkers came up to me and said, "Don't you know who that was?" I said I had no idea. He said it was J. C. Duke, one of 3M's vice presidents! My coworker went on to say that management, including Mr. William McKnight, the corporate CEO, liked to wander around and might show up anywhere at any time to talk with employees.

2.01 Value and Respect

My workday started at noon. With the help of my Hamline University advisor, Dr. Kent Bracewell, I was able to schedule my classes during the morning hours, which allowed me to put in a full eight hours at 3M during the afternoon and evening hours. One day, when I arrived at work, there was a group of people crowded into the area around my desk. I asked, "What's going on?" My supervisor, Mike Maloney, said they were honoring one of the secretaries for her product improvement idea and were rewarding her with a number of shares of 3M stock.

3M manufactured a variety of sanding belts for industrial applications. One in particular was a belt for sanding and polishing jet turbine blades. General Electric and others had complained that the belts rapidly frayed along the edges, reducing the efficiency, work quality, and useful life of the belts. When the secretary heard of the fraying problem, she went to the abrasive laboratory and showed them a number of fingernail files, the edges of which she had coated with a special brand of fingernail polish that kept them from fraying. Although the lab had been working on the problem, they hadn't found a satisfactory solution. Her idea worked!

All employees were encouraged to think of new ideas and if they came up with a useful one, they were recognized, honored, and occasionally rewarded like the secretary. William McKnight understood the value of encouraging employees to exercise their initiative and wrote a letter to management in 1948 defining the role of management at 3M. Copies of the letter could be found posted in various locations around the company.

"The Challenge of Management"
By William L. McKnight
1948

As our business grows, it becomes increasingly necessary to delegate responsibility and to encourage men and women to exercise their initiative. This requires considerable tolerance.

Those men and women, to whom we delegate authority and responsibility, if they are good people, are going to want to do their jobs in their own way. These characteristics we want, and people should be encouraged as long as their way conforms to our general pattern of operations.

Mistakes will be made, but if a person is essentially right, the mistakes he or she makes are not as serious, in the long run, as the mistakes management will make if it's dictatorial and undertakes to tell those under its authority exactly how they must do their jobs. Management that is destructively critical when mistakes are made kills initiative, and it is essential that we have many people with initiative if we are to grow.

On another occasion in 1955, I discovered a new machine had been installed near my desk. It was the newly developed Model 12 Thermofax copy machine. It was about the size of a washing machine and could make a copy of a letter or document in just a few seconds without the use of any chemicals. At the time, it was a revolutionary technology. It was the innovation and invention of Carl Miller. He and his laboratory asked us to use it, evaluate it, suggest new uses for it, and suggest improvements. This gave us the feeling that we were all working together to develop new products and help grow the company. Little did I know how much that machine would influence my life and my career at 3M.

3.00 New Business Innovation

The following section is a review of the innovation process freedom and practices at 3M that drove the development of new technologies and new markets and led to the establishment of a 3M new-to-the-world business. It spans the period of 1956 through 1964.

3.01 A Career in Innovation

After working for a year in the Abrasive Converting department, I had a conversation with our department manager, Carl Flegal. I expressed my interest in technical research and development. He arranged several interviews for me and within a week I had a new job as a lab technician in, of all places, the new Thermofax Project Laboratory. This was the first step in my 3M career that continued for more than forty years.

Two of my greatest mentors who shaped my career at 3M were Emil Grieshaber and Art Kotz.

Emil was one of my first supervisors, one of my greatest mentors, and also became my best friend. Although Emil had a PhD in organic chemistry, the first thing I learned from him was his name was Emil, not "Doctor." He expected a lot from everyone, and he got it. Although 3M didn't have a work/study policy at that time, he gave me the freedom to work around my class schedule.

Art was an outstanding mentor and teacher. He made technology interesting and fun. He took me under his wing as soon as I started work in the lab, providing much appreciated encouragement, guidance, advice and consultation.

3.02 The 15 Percent Rule

Each of us received research assignments with the objectives of improving the infrared copying technology and looking for new applications. Emil would frequently stop by the lab to review our progress. He always started the conversation with "What's new?" We knew that he expected an answer so we would rack our brains to find something "new" to show him. If we came up with an unrelated idea, he permitted us to work on it on "our own time." Our own time was our lunch time, our coffee breaks, and after hours.

A few years later, the company officially adopted this idea and named it the **"3M 15 percent rule"** which states that, ***"Regardless of their assignments, 3M technical employees are encouraged to devote 15 percent of their working hours to independent projects."***

The 15 percent rule is unique to 3M. Frequently unexpected new phenomena and new ideas are discovered that can lead to new opportunities. This rule makes it possible for employees with initiative to pursue their ideas that may otherwise be discarded or forgotten. Most of the inventions that have built 3M are the result of the 15 percent rule.

3.03 Opportunity Analysis

Friday afternoons were reserved for "show-and-tell" time.

Emil supplied coffee and doughnuts, and we would spend the rest of the afternoon reviewing, discussing, analyzing, and promoting our "own time" ideas and "new" discoveries. The questions raised at the show and tell included technical issues, manufacturability, customer need, potential market size, business opportunities, and more.

3M pioneered the copying, or duplicating, industry with the development of the thermographic imaging process. For the first time in history, a copy of a document could be made in a few seconds without the need for chemicals and cameras. However, it was blind to colored images on the original, and only black infrared absorbing images could be copied.

To solve this problem, we replaced the infrared energy source or lamp with an intense source of visible energy— a Xenon flash lamp. However, this required an intermediate copy film that was transparent to the visible light energy. The transparent intermediate copy film was placed on an original and exposed to the flash lamp in the coping machine. The intermediate film was then placed on a plain sheet of paper and passed through the copying machine a second time. This transferred the image created on the intermediate copy film to the plain paper, producing a permanent black-and-white copy of the original.

Using visible light as the primary energy source, colored images could be reproduced in black and white for the first time. The system was marketed as the "3M Model 26 Check Copier" and was used by banks to copy

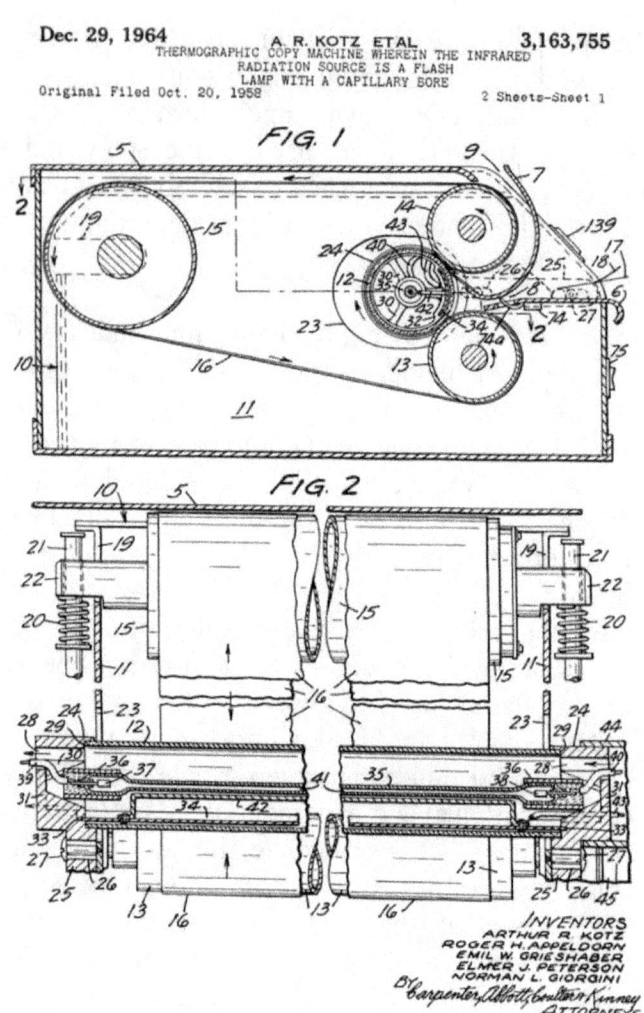

3M Model 26 Check Copier Patent

endorsed checks and other legal documents containing colored ink images.

We didn't like throwing the intermediate film away, so

we started to look for other possible uses for the film. We found that we could project it onto a screen using a "view-graph projector" that had been developed to project 8 x 10" Air Force aerial surveillance photographs during the 1940s. However, the projected image was poor due to the brownish tint and translucent nature of the intermediate copy film.

While attempting to improve the clarity of the intermediate copy film, I discovered a new thermographic imaging process. The surface of an optically clear oriented (i.e., thermally stretched) plastic film was first treated with a chemical penetrant that would sever the oriented polymer chains on the surface. When heated in the image areas, the severed polymer chains would shrink and form a dense white image on the surface that scattered light. Although the image appeared white on the transparency, it produced a jet-black image against a clear white background when projected onto a screen.

Shortly after I demonstrated the new imaging system, a man in a business suit showed up—looking for me. It was the 3M corporate president, A. G. Bush. He had heard about my discovery and had taken time out of his schedule to come to our lab and see what I had done. Was I impressed! Imagine the president of the company taking an interest in what *I* was doing. There are no words that describe the impact this simple act on his part had on me.

3.04 Make-a-Little, Sell-a-Little

The Friday afternoon show-and-tell group concluded that there must be a market for this new copy film, so we introduced it to the sales and marketing group. To our surprise, they didn't think much of it and turned us down.

Undaunted, we made our own sales call. We made enough transparency film to fill five boxes, each with one hundred sheets of film, and labeled them "3M Type 123 Viewgraph Transparency Film" to make it look very official.

One evening, on the way home from work, Don Newman, Dick Jones, and I stopped to see Emma Storstein, the audio-visual director for the North Saint Paul, Minnesota, school system. She was so impressed that she bought our entire supply of transparency film (all five boxes) and ordered several Thermofax copy machines to boot.

The next morning, with the order in hand, we proudly met with the sales and marketing group—again. This time they agreed to market and sell the transparency film.

A few months later, I received a call from Colonel Tally at the SAC Air Force Base in Omaha, Nebraska. He was in charge of the war room where daily briefings using view graph projectors were held with the Generals. He had heard about our new transparency film and wanted a demonstration. When his staff saw how fast we could make a transparency of an original and project it onto the briefing room screen, they bought our system and began using over twenty thousand sheets of transparency copy film a month in the SAC underground control center. Soon, other military bases all around the world began to use it as well.

The 3M Model 45 "Secretary" Copy Machine

We had the Thermofax copying machine and a line of transparency films, but we needed a Viewgraph Projector to offer a complete line of products. We contracted with an optical company (Buhl Optics) in Pittsburgh, Pennsylvania, to manufacture one for us. This was the Model 42, our first viewgraph projector.

3M Model 42 Viewgraph Projector

3.05 Vision

Now that sales were significant, we asked ourselves, "Where are we really going with this system?" From early on, we were convinced the system provided a much better meeting and educational tool than did a blackboard and chalk. We decided that the large education market *needed* this technology, and it should therefore be our primary target. (To promote our vision, we changed the words to the song "Bye Bye Bluebird" to "Bye Bye Blackboard" and had fun singing it at our sales and marketing meetings.)

Our vision was to revolutionize the meeting room and education process through the introduction and marketing of the viewgraph projector and visual transparency system.

One day, a local 3M salesman called me and invited me to make a few sales calls with him. We spent the entire day making sales calls, and he made it my job to carry and set up the viewgraph projector.

First, its 1960 price of $495 was out of reach for most customers. The Viewgraph frequently required dimming the room lights to project a bright enough image on the screen. Second, that projector weighed around sixty pounds, not including the wheeled case, which was a 3 x 2.5 x 1.5' box. Worse yet, all the sales calls were on the third or fourth floor of the buildings! The salesman wanted to make sure that I got the message, and I got it. It was a neat product, but what the market really needed was a lighter-weight, smaller, brighter, and lower-cost overhead projector.

Our first try at developing a new projector was a failure. The optics and numerous extra features and functions the marketing department insisted on drove the cost way out of sight. In addition, the marketing department had hired a market research firm to study the market. After spending over $200,000 (in 1960 dollars), they concluded that the market for the projector was relatively small and that what the people really *wanted* was a better blackboard and not a projector and transparency system. With the results of that study and the projected cost of the proposed projector, management decided to shelve the project.

We were devastated. Later that day in mid-October 1961, we had a rather heated discussion with Bert Auger, our new project manager. We argued that the education market wasn't looking for a projector with all the extra features (we called them "whips, whistles, and balloons") but a brighter, lightweight, smaller, simpler, and much less expensive projector that was easy to use. Bert went back to the division management and convinced it to postpone shutting down the project for ninety days. However, at the end of ninety days, management wanted to "see" a working demonstration of our proposed low-cost projector. Dick Hipp (our mechanical designer), Lionel Schwartz (my technician), and I accepted the challenge, and the demonstration date of the new design was set for January 15, 1962.

3.06 Product Development Innovation

We tried to use a low-cost meniscus lens, known as a landscape lens, as the projection lens to reduce the cost. But due to its inherent optical aberrations, the projected image was fuzzy and had low contrast.

I had been studying the properties of echelon lenses (frequently referred to as Fresnel lenses) and realized that they held the key to the development of the projector we had proposed. The echelon lens has a series of circular prism-shaped grooves on its surface, each angled to replicate the surface angle of a continuous surface lens at a corresponding radius. The echelon lens is thin, lightweight, and low cost.

More importantly, the angle of each groove could be independently varied to correct for the other optical aberrations present in the system. This approach not only dramatically improved the performance of the landscape lens; it also improved the light collection efficiency of the entire optical system.

A precision micromachining capability is needed to create the original or master echelon lens. The master echelon lens is then replicated using a rather complex precision-molding process. However, the type of echelon lens with varied prism grooves required for our new projector had never been produced before. Our purchasing department couldn't locate a manufacturer that would even attempt manufacturing it. Our only option was to learn how to produce these lenses at 3M.

Another key element the projector needed was a revolutionary projection lamp. At that time, all projection lamps had to be operated in a vertical orientation with the light exiting the side of the lamp. The lamps could not be operated in a horizontal position because the tungsten evaporating from the filament would condense on the inside surface of the lamp bulb, above the filament, and block the light. We needed a lamp that would operate in the horizontal position to eliminate the extra lenses and mirrors normally used to redirect the light up toward the echelon lens and transparency stage.

General Electric had recently introduced a newer and brighter "tungsten-halogen" flood lamp. Iodine was added to the fill gas surrounding the filament. The iodine reacted with the evaporating tungsten, preventing it from condensing on the inside surface of the bulb. When the newly formed tungsten-iodide gas came in contact with the hot filament, the gas decomposed, redepositing the tungsten on the filament, keeping the bulb surface clean as well as increasing the life of the lamp.

This technology was the answer to our prayers! We asked GE to make sample projection lamps for us using this technology. However, it refused, saying that projection lamp filaments were not compatible with the halogen cycle. Try as we may, we couldn't get GE to even attempt it. So, we decided to make our own projection lamps.

Dick Peterson, a technician working in our laboratory, had learned how to make experimental infrared lamps for Thermofax copying machines. He went to work for us, and in a couple of weeks produced the world's first working halogen projection lamp. It operated in the horizontal position (eliminating the need for the extra mirrors and lenses), didn't darken with age, and lasted many times longer than conventional projection lamps.

We demonstrated our new lamp to GE. It was shocked. It had no idea we would have the ability to make our own lamps. Our division manager, Ray Herzog, suggested that if GE wasn't interested in making the projection lamp, 3M would. It's amazing how quickly attitudes can change. From then on, we got the most amazing service from GE. Within days of the meeting, GE supplied us with dozens of different experimental lamps for evaluation.

The existing Viewgraph projectors were bulky and heavy; they had ten or more optical elements, 500-watt projection lamps and bulky, expensive, and relatively loud cooling systems. Our new design, the "3M Overhead Projector," had only three different inexpensive optical elements, a simple, relatively quiet cooling system, and a revolutionary 300-watt tungsten-halogen (iodine) projection lamp. The new design was one-fifth the weight, twice as bright, quiet, and one-fourth the manufacturing cost of the existing Viewgraph projectors.

On January 15, 1962, we demonstrated our prototype overhead projector to management. It was a hit. The good news was that we got the go-ahead and the project was saved. The bad news was that management wanted the projector to be in full production by August 12 of that year! The plan was to introduce and deliver projectors to retail dealers at the annual 3M national dealer meeting in Florida. If we missed that date, we would be forced to delay its introduction for an entire year. We had only seven months to scale up manufacturing for the new projector as well as develop a process to produce the new echelon lens.

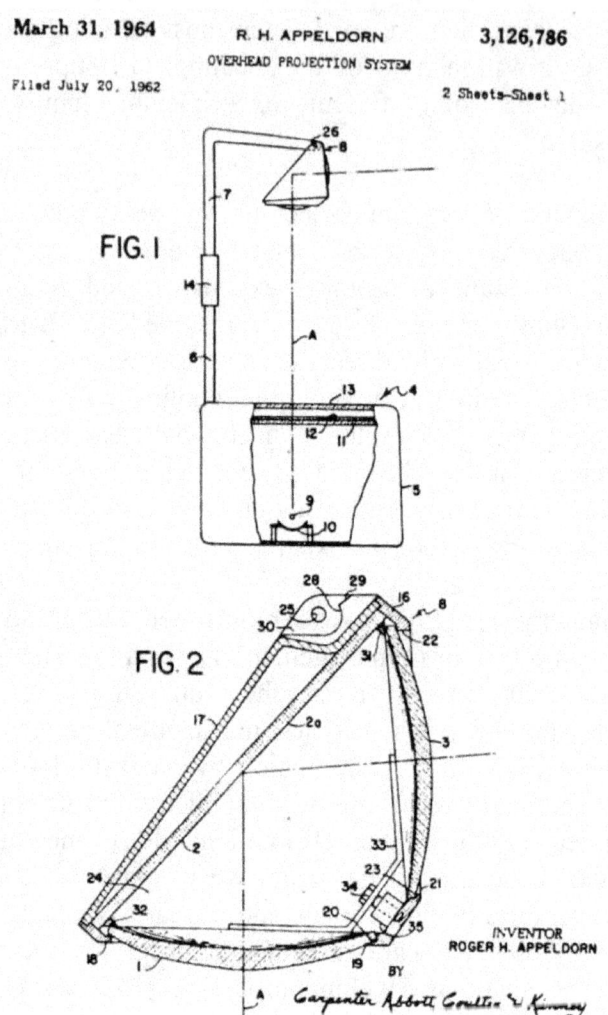

The 3M Model 66 Overhead Projector Patent

30

3.07 Innovating around Rules

I immediately started the process of hiring the people we would need to complete the design and scale up manufacturing. However, I ran smack dab into a company-wide hiring freeze. I wasn't allowed to hire anybody!

While lamenting over this dilemma with our purchasing agent, Dick Hewitt, he suggested that all we really needed were the design prints and manufacturing specifications. So, why not go outside the company, contract with an engineering firm, and have them produce the prints and specifications we required? All we would need was a purchase requisition to pay for the finished prints and specifications. We wouldn't need to hire anyone.

The plan worked, but we tired of driving back and forth several times a day to the engineering firms, which were located on the other side of the Twin Cities. So, we invited the engineering firms to locate their engineers and designers at our 3M facility to complete their work. We agreed to provide temporary passes, desks, and some of the tools they would need and put them in an unused conference room that happened to be available. Before long, the engineering firms had assigned fifteen or more people to our project and we didn't need a single employment requisition!

I continued to use this design approach for several years—before I got caught. When management discovered what I was doing, it created quite a stir all the way up to the 3M Board of Directors.

I was summarily "invited" to explain my actions to Bob Adams, vice president of Research and Development. After listening to a lengthy lecture about how I had broken the company's rules and policies, I asked Bob what I might have done differently—considering the circumstances. Bob leaned forward and quietly said: "Your mistake was getting caught!" Later, when the Board of Directors reviewed the situation, our CEO William McKnight said "Just let him do his job."

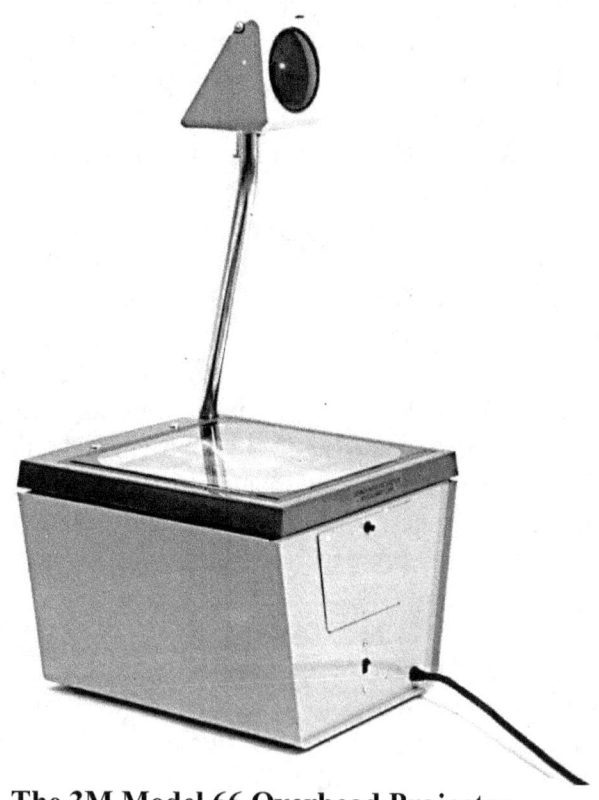

The 3M Model 66 Overhead Projector

The design was completed, and production, coordinated by Jim Warmack, started on time. The dealer show in Florida was a hit, initial sales took off, and we sold out our entire inventory at the show. But to our dismay, sales suddenly slowed down. The schools and teachers just weren't buying it. The problem was that schools didn't have the money to spend, and the teachers didn't *want* to change their teaching techniques and methods. They were used to using the old blackboard.

3.08 Innovation Contributors

Sales had grown enough that we became a department, which entitled us to have our own accountant. One day, when reviewing the status of the business, our manager Bert Auger lamented and said, "The only way we will get projectors into the schools is by giving them away!"

Our accountant, Frank Lucas, said, "Why not?" A gift to the schools would be considered a charitable donation, which at that time entitled 3M to a tax deduction equal to the market value of the product. This meant that the tax deduction for the corporation would more than cover the manufacturing cost of the projector. Further, all these projectors would promote the additional sale of transparencies and Thermofax copying machines. We had an innovative accountant!

The plan was implemented, and we titled it "AGE," or "Assistance Grant to Education." To receive a grant of projectors, an educational institution or school was required to submit a plan describing how it would use and integrate the projector and transparencies into the classroom. A panel of non-3M judges reviewed the proposals and selected those worthy of grants. When we announced the program, we were immediately swamped with literally thousands of applications. We couldn't give the projectors away fast enough.

3.09 Innovation Fruition

The program was a success. Each succeeding year had a different focus. **AGE I** focused on high school education, **AGE II** focused on middle school education, and **AGE III** focused on elementary education. After the third year, the tax rules were changed, limiting a tax deduction to the actual manufacturing cost of the projector. However, by that time the market had been established, a whole new business had been created, and we saw our vision become a reality. By 1964, sales exceeded $50 million (in 1964 dollars) with profits in excess of 20 percent, and the Visual Products department was named a 3M division.

4.00 Technology Innovation

The development of the 3M overhead projector echelon lens and the innovative processes to manufacture it led to the identification of a new science. This became the foundation for the creation of a corporate technology platform that was named "microreplication." The following describes some of the developments, activities, programs, events, etc., that drove the formation of this platform as well as the development of a multitude of diverse new-to-the-world products and businesses. This section spans the period of 1964 through 1995.

4.01 Expanding the Product Line

After the successful introduction of the 3M overhead projector and overhead transparency film, our attention turned to expanding the product line of our division. A broad line of copy films for making overhead transparencies was developed under the direction of Don Newman. We also developed low-cost compact copy machines or "transparency makers." In addition, a new style of overhead projector, the 3M Model 88, was developed using reflective echelon lens technology.

Overhead projectors like the 3M Model 66 positioned the projection lamp in a housing below the projection stage. This is so the light would be directed up through the projection stage and through the projection transparency. As a result, the projection stage was about eight to ten inches above the table or stand upon which the projector was placed. Also, placing the projection lamp below the stage required cooling the housing and lamp with a fan that made noise.

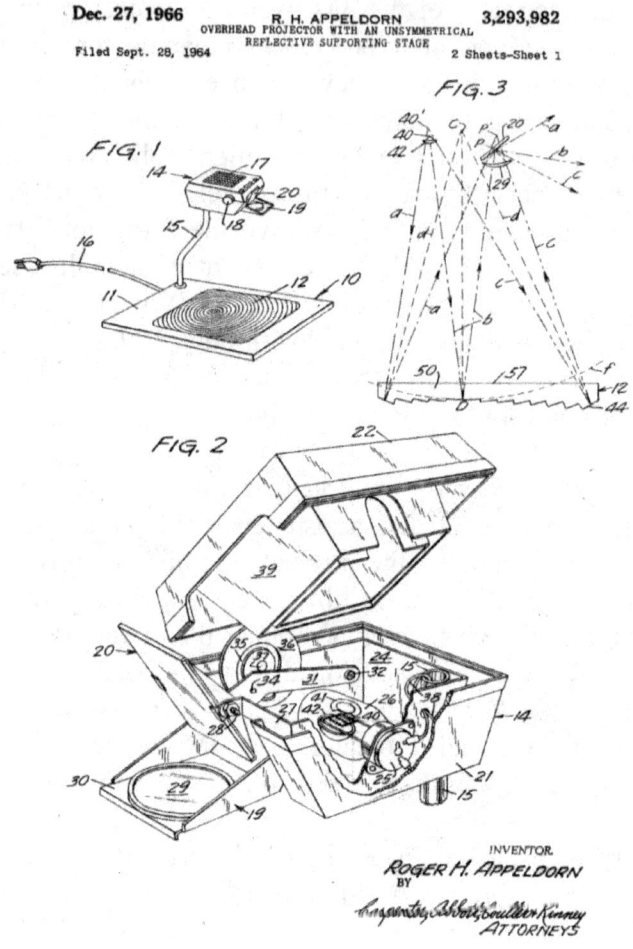

Dec. 27, 1966   R. H. APPELDORN   3,293,982
OVERHEAD PROJECTOR WITH AN UNSYMMETRICAL
REFLECTIVE SUPPORTING STAGE
Filed Sept. 28, 1964   2 Sheets—Sheet 1

FIG. 1
FIG. 2
FIG. 3

INVENTOR.
ROGER H. APPELDORN
BY
ATTORNEYS

The Model 088 Overhead Projector

The 3M Model 088 Overhead Projector used a "reflective" echelon lens as the projection stage. The projection lamp was positioned alongside the projection lens, above the projection stage. This directed light downward, through the transparency on the stage, which was a reflective echelon lens. The reflective echelon lens reflected the light back through the transparency and into the projection lens. The result was a projector with a projection stage only one inch high above a table or desk it was placed upon. Because the lamp was above the projection stage, it could be air cooled, thus eliminating the need for a noisy cooling fan. The projector was completely quiet. Since the housing below the projection stage was eliminated, the projector could be folded into a compact package about the size of a medium-size briefcase, thus making it truly portable. The projector became a very popular item for education as well as for commercial applications, and it was one of our most popular and profitable products.

4.02 New and Unrelated Product and Business Development

3M divisions annually reviewed their business objectives, plans, and statuses with corporate management each year in October. In addition to reviewing their core business, each division was expected to review their new and unrelated product development programs. Development of new and unrelated business opportunities would ensure the continued growth and prosperity of the divisions and the company. In complying with this expectation, we began to look for other new and unique uses for our new echelon lens technology. The following are some examples.

Internally Illuminated Signs

A sister division, Reflective Products (later renamed Traffic Control Products), marketed retroreflective sheeting that used glass beads on its surface to enhance the visibility of highway signs and road markings by reflecting a portion of the light from the automotive headlights back toward the driver, (i.e., "retroreflective"). To expand the market for the beaded sheeting, Reflective Products acquired National Advertising Inc., a company that marketed, erected, and leased outdoor advertising signs along highways, on buildings, etc. The use of the retroreflective sheeting enhanced the performance of outdoor advertising signs, broadening the use of the retroreflective sheeting.

National Advertising expressed an interest in internally illuminated signs to expand their business. However, illuminated signs consumed a great deal of power and many, if not most, sign locations had no source of electricity. They were looking for a system that would require little power or that could be powered with batteries if necessary.

Using an echelon lens about one foot square and with a focal length of one foot, we constructed a sign six feet high and twelve feet wide using an array of seventy-two lenses. A low-wattage lamp with a diffuse white surface was placed at the focal point of each lens. When viewed from the front, the entire sign appeared very bright and uniformly illuminated. The total power consumption was less than one hundred watts. However, the illuminated viewing angle of the sign was only about eight degrees. When one moved outside of the viewing angle, the entire sign went dark. This was considered unacceptable, and due to the complex construction, the idea was shelved.

Optical Guidance Systems

At about this time, we became aware of the United States Air Force's need for a system that would accurately guide aircraft dropping supplies into war zones at night. Because they couldn't use the normal communication systems or ground lighting, the pilot and navigator of the cargo plane were forced to use dead reckoning to find the drop zone. This was very inaccurate, and they had difficulty dropping the supplies within a thousand-foot radius of the designated drop zone. This resulted in supplies not only missing the target but even falling into enemy hands.

Using an echelon lens similar to the lens designed for the internally illuminated sign project, we developed an optical guidance device and system. The echelon lens projected a coded optical beam from the drop zone toward the aircraft. The diffuse white lamp used in the sign described above was replaced with a light source consisting of a small tungsten lamp, several colored filters, and several small xenon flash lamps powered by two AA-size batteries. The optical beam of light created by the echelon lens and the coded light source gave the aircraft navigator guidance information such as the distance to the drop zone, aircraft altitude, approach angle, etc. Although visible from the air, the device was nearly impossible to see or detect from the ground. The device was given the acronym of NAVIGS, or "Night Aerial Visually Illuminated Guidance System."

To test NAVIGS, we enlisted a couple of former Air Force pilots to fly over the device and test its visibility and guidance accuracy. We positioned one of the devices in a wooded area twenty-five miles north of Saint Paul, Minnesota. There were numerous residential lights, car lights, and yard lights in the area, and we became concerned that the pilots wouldn't be able to see it at all. While describing the coded light beam, how it worked, and what to look for to the pilots during take-off, one of the pilots interrupted me and said, "Never mind, I already see it," and we were still over twenty miles away.

The next test was at Fort Bragg, North Carolina. This time it was a real air-drop test. Again, the pilot and navigator were able to immediately pick out the device as soon as we were in the air proceeding toward the drop zone. We had planned to test drop loads from five different planes. I was in the lead plane, and we dropped our load using the optical guidance signals. The second plane followed and also dropped its load using the NAVIGS optical guidance information. Suddenly, we received a frantic call from the drop zone on the ground ordering that all air drops cease. The accuracy of the device was so good that the loads were landing on top of one another!

The Air Force qualified and accepted the device, classifying it as "secret." Although I know 3M continued to supply lenses and light packages for several years, that was the last we heard of it.

Optically Programmed Traffic Signals
One day while driving down a street near the 3M center, I

approached an intersection newly equipped with traffic signal lights. There were signal lights for the through lanes as well as for the left-turn lanes. The left-turn lane signal light would turn green, allowing cars to turn left, while the through lane signal lights remained red, halting the through traffic. A car in the through lane in front of me saw the left-turn signal light turn green. Thinking the left-turn signal was for him, he drove into the intersection and collided with a car that was legally turning left. Although it was a very loud fender bender, fortunately no one was seriously hurt.

The highway and street departments attempted to use shields to limit the visibility of the left-turn light to only those in the left turn lane. However, shields were not very successful due to the proximity of the left-turn lane to the through lane. Signs explaining what lane the stop lights regulated were largely unnoticed or ignored by drivers. What was needed was a traffic signal that could only be seen by the cars in the lane or lanes it regulated.

I developed a traffic signal using the echelon lens. When mounted in an intersection, the echelon lens projected an image of the traffic lanes onto a glass window behind the lens. Opaque tape was applied to the window, covering the image of the traffic lanes that should not see the signal, and leaving the window clear where the signal should be seen. A lamp was then placed behind the window to illuminate the traffic signal. The result was a signal that when lit would only be seen in the traffic lanes the signal controlled.

This became the 3M Model 131 optically programmed

traffic signal program championed by two incredibly innovative people, Joe Fitzpatrick and Craig Leiser.

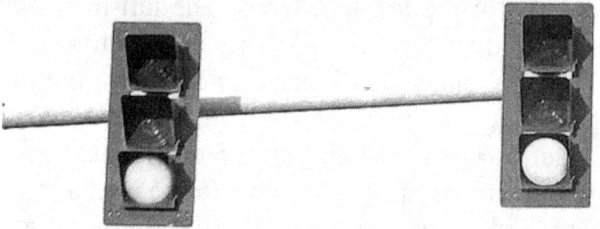

3M Model 131 traffic signal as seen from the lane it controls.

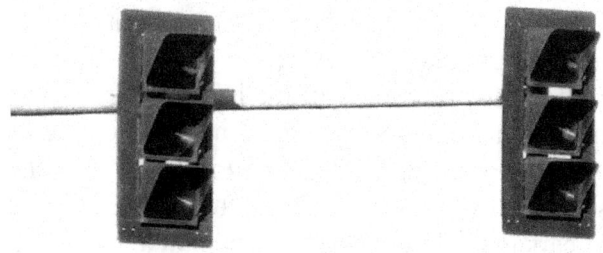

3M Model 131 traffic signal as seen in an adjacent lane it does not control.

Intersections equipped with this signal dramatically reduced congestion and accidents. A typical example was at an intersection near Los Angeles, California, where three streets came together at a single intersection. Drivers were so confused by the multitude of signal lights that several accidents occurred there every day. After the Model 131 signals were installed, accidents at the intersection were all but eliminated. The improvement was so dramatic that the state of California subsequently required all intersections with left-turn lanes to be equipped with the Model 131. This eventually led to the formation of a new Traffic Control Devices Department business unit.

Automotive Headlights

An improved automotive headlamp system was also developed using the unique echelon lens. At the time, the standard automotive headlamp was a sealed-beam construction that had limited optical performance—it did not adequately illuminate the roadway and it restricted the design flexibility of the automotive designers. The headlamp we created with the echelon lens was not restricted to round or square shapes and could be tailored to accommodate the automotive designers. The echelon lens uniformly distributed the light emanating from the light source over its entire surface, which greatly reduced the glare to oncoming motorists. This allowed us to significantly increase the roadway illumination without increasing the glare to oncoming drivers.

However, after considerable development, testing, and investment on our part, we discovered that Ford and General Motors had no intention of utilizing our headlamp technology in the foreseeable future. They had recently invested in a new sealed-beam headlight manufacturing facility in Indiana and had no intention of abandoning the sealed-beam headlight design until that capital investment had been paid off, which would be many years in the future. They really didn't *need* the new technology. We cancelled the project.

My Own 15 Percent Project

Our micromachining capability for producing echelon lenses advanced to the point that we were able to create more complex microtopographies. Of special interest was the machining of an array of cube corners to create a retroreflector. A cube corner is an optical element with three reflective optical faces that are mutually perpendicular to one another. A light ray from a distant light source, such as an automotive headlight, entering a cube corner will be reflected three times. Upon the third reflection, the light ray is rendered parallel to the incoming light ray and returns toward the automobile headlight, regardless of its location relative to the cube corner.

3M had developed a retroreflective sheeting using arrays of reflectorized glass beads on an adhesive sheet or substrate. The glass bead acts as a lens that collects the incoming light and reflects it off the back side of the bead, which returns it back through the bead and toward the light source, thus creating a retroreflector. However, the manufacturing process was highly complex, expensive, and the overall retroreflective efficiency was relatively low.

Cube corners were known to be many times more efficient than glass-bead retroreflectors. Products using cube-corner elements were available but limited to small-injection molded discs or buttons. If large-area cube-corner sheeting could be produced using the echelon lens technology, it would provide better optical performance, a more durable product, a simplified manufacturing process, and an overall reduction in manufacturing cost.

Another significant advantage of the cube-corner optical element over glass-bead technology is the ability to control the return angle of the retroreflected light. If all the light is perfectly retroreflected, the light would return to the headlight and the sign would appear dark to the driver. Physical errors and optical aberrations in the glass-bead optics slightly scatter the retroreflected light through a range of angles, making some of it visible to the driver. In a cube-corner retroreflector, the angles of the reflective faces can be altered to direct more of the light toward the driver rather than back toward the light source.

Our division manager, Bert Auger, initially objected to my exploration of this technology. He said: "That is a job for Reflective Products, not for you." I couldn't get Reflective Products interested, so I made the study of cube-corner optics a personal hobby, working on it in the evenings and on weekends. A mathematical modeling technique was developed that predicted the optical result when the reflective faces were tilted or rotated through any predetermined angle.

This led to my discovery that complex optical patterns and even optical images could be created by the retroreflected beam through the angular control of the prism face orientation and configuration. I also discovered that it was possible to machine a master where each individual cube-corner element in the array would have a unique and different optical design and property. This made it possible to manage the retroreflected beam and provide more uniform and brighter sign visibility to the motorist.

Using our echelon manufacturing technology, a demonstration master was machined from which we produced the first large-area flexible cube-corner retroreflector. I demonstrated the samples to Don Douglas, vice president of the Reflective Products Division. Although he was impressed with the samples, he said they had little interest at the time because they had just made a substantial investment in the development and introduction of "high-intensity sheeting," an improved glass-bead retroreflective product.

Word got around about some of our optical developments and I received a call from 3M's president and CEO, Harry Heltzer. He said he wanted to see a demonstration of our new optical technology. Lasers were just coming into use and we had been using a laser to illustrate how the overhead projector optics and other echelon lenses worked. Believing he wanted to see the laser demonstration, I packed up the equipment and samples and headed for his office. On the way out of the door, I grabbed one of the cube-corner retroreflector samples—just in case.

It turned out that Harry was most interested in the new cube-corner retroreflector. After I demonstrated it to him, he asked if I had shown it to Don Douglas. I said that I had. Harry then asked, "What did Don say?" I replied that Don said he wasn't interested in it at this time since they had just introduced "high-intensity sheeting." Harry looked at me, smiled, and said, "He is now!" and sure enough, I got a call from Don later that afternoon asking that I call a meeting to review the new cube-corner development program.

Harry Heltzer attended the meeting and asked to speak first. He said that all products have a lifetime and that sooner or later, competition or competitive technology would catch up to overtake your current product, rendering it obsolete. The time to invest in new technology and new products is now, when we have the lead. If you wait until it is needed, it will be too late!

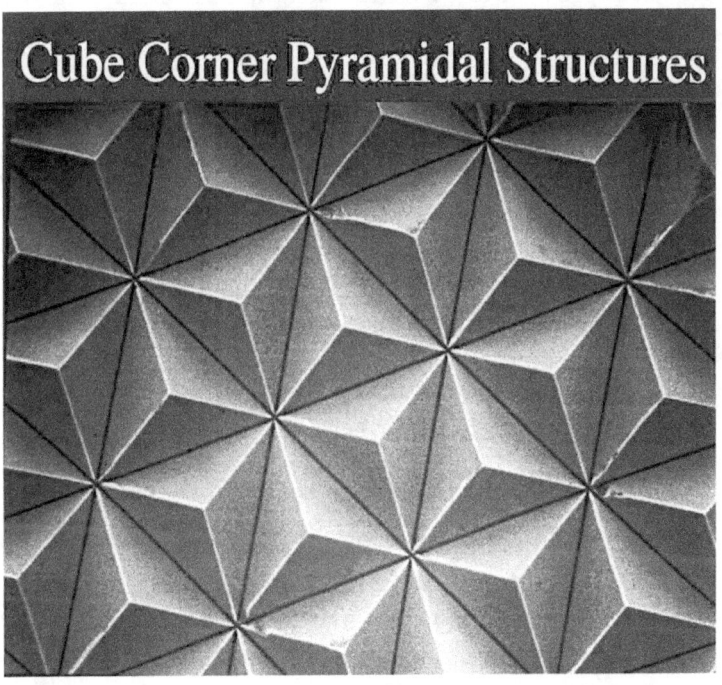

Cube-Corner Retroreflective Sheeting

This initiated a fifteen-year program to develop, manufacture, and introduce cube-corner retroreflective sheeting (as well as other structured-surface products) made by the yard.

4.03 Seeds for a New Technology

Additional applications for the echelon lenses were being found, including digital LED magnifiers for watches and micrographic optical systems, for example. The echelon lens was proving to be more versatile and useful than we had originally imagined.

In principle, the echelon lens is a relatively thin, transparent sheet with a precision surface topography that changes or modifies its optical properties. The topography could be a series of circular or linear prismatic-like grooves or even an array of individual optical pixels, each with a unique topography that had a predetermined optical function or property. We called the technology "incremental" or "digital" optics.

The basic process of manufacturing sheets or films with incremental optics properties involved the following:

1. **Micromachining a master mold with the desired topography.**
   Micromachining the master mold required highly specialized machining equipment with ultra-precise mechanical accuracy and stability. Machining tolerances in the range of "millionths of an inch" were required. To maintain cutting accuracy, single-crystalline diamond cutting tools were used to minimize tool wear and maintain the cutting precision. The topography was machined

onto the surface of a master, which could be a metal such as brass or aluminum. We preferred polymethyl methacrylate because of its chemical and physical stability and ease of machining.

2. **Replicating the master in metal to create the molding tool.**

Replicating the master in a metal mold required precision-electroforming technology. The process involved depositing a thin, conductive film, such as silver, onto the master and then electro-depositing a thicker metal layer, usually nickel, on top of the silver.

One of the difficulties we encountered was getting the silver to adhere to the master. Conventional technology called for chemically etching the surface to ensure the silver would adhere to the master. However, this technique severely degraded the optical quality of the surface. A breakthrough came one day when Harlan Krinke, who was researching and developing the needed electro-forming technology, discovered a remarkable surface treatment that greatly improved the adhesion of the silver to the master without degrading its optical surface quality at all. In addition, the treatment, which became known as "Harlan's pickle juice," made it possible to replicate masters made from a variety of polymers and other substrates as well.

After a sufficient metal thickness is electroplated onto the silver surface, the master is separated from the electroplated metal, resulting in a negative metal copy of the master. This metal copy of the master is referred to as the "mother." Metal, such as nickel, was subsequently deposited onto the "mother" to produce the final production molding tool replica.

3. **Molding the tool topography onto a sheet or film.**
   The molding-tool replica is then used to compression mold the surface topography onto or in the surface of the final article or product. This is known as a "batch process." It was our dream, however, to develop a continuous molding process with these tools and to make "lenses by the yard"—but that was to come later.

4.04 Discovering a New Technical Platform

While developing the manufacturing processes, we discovered that the technology was much broader and not limited to the manufacturing of optical articles. For example, we created a replica of a microsurface topography we had machined, known as a "moth's eye," the topography of which was a sinusoidal undulating surface with peaks and valleys only a fraction of the wavelength of light in height. This surface eliminated surface reflections and the need for antireflection coatings.

Harlan discovered that this surface also changed the chemical and physical properties of the surface as well. One day, he came running into my office with several samples of polyethylene and Teflon film with the moth's eye topography molded on their surfaces. Both materials were widely known for their "anti-adhesive" or "nonstick" properties but when an adhesive tape was applied to Harlan's samples, the adhesion was so great that when attempting to remove the tape from the surface, the adhesive pulled away from the tape backing and remained firmly anchored on the surface of polyethylene and Teflon samples.

Harlan, other people in the lab and I soon discovered other topographies that changed the hydrophilic (water wetting) or hydrophobic (water repelling) properties of a material's surface. We also demonstrated that numerous physical, chemical, electrical, and optical properties of a material's surface could be altered or controlled in many useful ways by molding the appropriate topography on the surface.

Exploring these discoveries, we suddenly realized that a common thread ran through or connected the various technologies we were developing and using. The concepts of incremental optics, digital optics, structured materials, and surfaces all involved

> *creating and reproducing precision micro structures within or on the surface of a material that are designed to modify or change the physical, mechanical, chemical, or optical properties of that material.*

Later, this technology was given the title: "3M microreplication."

4.05 Defining a New Business Project

We received a call from the 3M corporate office. It had learned that the owners of Polacoat Inc., an optical company located in Blue Ash, Ohio, was for sale and looking to be acquired. The company produced and marketed a line of optical products, including a line of rear-projection screens, liquid-crystal polarizers, and other liquid-crystal products. It appeared there would be a fit with our growing interest in optical film technology and products. In addition, our sister division, Micrographic Products, used the screens in their microfilm readers and printers.

Polacoat Inc. was founded by John Dryer. Its first products were polarizing glasses for viewing 3D movies that they made using a unique liquid-crystal and coating technology. Their coating process led to a number of other light-polarizing products as well as a complete line of rear-projection screens. It had pioneered the development and patented a number of liquid-crystal materials and products that included the liquid-crystal chemicals, liquid-crystal displays, light switches, and a variety of ultrasound sensing films.

To function as a display or light switch, liquid-crystal molecules need to be oriented or aligned on a surface or within the device. This was accomplished by introducing a linear microtopography on the surface of the substrate that holds or encapsulates the liquid crystal. The linear microtopography forces the liquid-crystal molecules to align with the surface topography so that their polarizing properties can be utilized. Here was another technology that could benefit from our microstructured surface technology.

We acquired the company and their technology. Our business plan was as follows:

1. Manufacture rear small projection screens for the 3M Micrographic Products Division.
2. Market large rear projection screens for overhead projectors through the Visual Production Division.
3. Combine the screen business and other Polacoat optical products with our own optical and structured surface products to form a new business development project. The project was titled "Industrial Optics."
4. Initiate research projects in Industrial Optics and the Visual Products divisions to develop improved liquid-crystal chemicals, materials, and display panels, and develop an electronic overhead projector utilizing liquid crystal technology.

4.06 Expanding Opportunity Analysis Skills

The University of Minnesota offered a short course titled Financial Management for Non-Financial Managers. The instructor was Richard Cardozo, a former Proctor and Gamble executive and at the time a professor at the Carlson School of Management. I took his week-long course, which turned out to be one of the most valuable courses I have ever taken. Cardozo's focus was on evaluating new business opportunities without investing a lot of time or money on market research studies.

Cardozo started by saying that P&G could not afford to conduct market research studies and surveys for every new product it was developing, nor was it necessary. He told us, "You already know all you need to know!" To illustrate, he introduced the class to a number of new innovations that had already been reduced to practice, and it was our job to estimate the business opportunity and develop a financial business model for each one. He broke the class into teams of six to eight people, giving each team about two hours to estimate the business opportunity and develop a financial model for the product he assigned to us for analysis. We had no access to libraries or research materials. We were forced to rely solely on our own experiences and personal knowledge (i.e., "what we already know"). Each team would then present their analysis of the business opportunity for that product, and then Cardozo would disclose what had actually happened to that product and the business in the real world.

We were amazed how accurate our estimates were with respect to what had actually happened in the real world. Cardozo emphasized that this approach of market analysis is not precise, but neither are formal surveys nor market studies. A high level of precision is not important in analyzing business opportunities. What is important is establishing a viability or usefulness measure of the proposed product and business opportunity and discerning whether or not it is worth investing in it.

4.07 Applying Opportunity Analysis

Following the acquisition of Polacoat, we analyzed our

fundamental technology, capabilities, and innovations to develop an understanding of the business opportunity for our microreplication and microstructured technologies and capabilities. A number of the project members, including Ray Anderson, Sandy Cobb, Terry Jones, and I met to evaluate the business opportunity utilizing the techniques taught by Richard Cardozo.

It was concluded that our uniqueness and strength lie in the design and manufacture of optical films, technologies, and materials. Our overall **vision** was to *develop a variety of relatively thin films possessing unique optical and nonoptical properties to enhance the performance of products or systems.* Although we identified numerous markets and applications that could use these unique optical films, three with the most promising potential stood out:

1. Electronic display image management and enhancement
2. Light and illumination management
3. Radiant energy management (e.g., solar collectors, concentrators, etc.)

Electronic displays were rated the most significant opportunity in the near term for several reasons:

1. Imaging technology was shifting from chemical to electronic technology, such as VCRs that were already replacing film movie cameras and were projected to replace the film still cameras as well. The need to display electronic images would drive the development of digital-electronic optical

displays.

2. With the development of liquid-crystal technology, flat-panel electronic optical displays were on the horizon. Having worked with the liquid-crystal technology, we were aware of the need for optical films for image enhancement and light management of the display.

3. Word processing systems or computers using digital CRT displays were already replacing typewriters and paper. Based upon the number of typewriters in use, we estimated that as word processors replaced typewriters, the square feet of word processing displays would require billions of square feet of films. It didn't matter how many billion, one billion was big enough!

We were faced with a short term problem, however. Our technology and capability preceded the market and it would be years before the market would develop the need for our technology. Our strategy was to focus on existing display applications such as CRTs, rear projection systems, and other optical applications, stay abreast of the emerging electronic display market, and ensure that we would be ready to supply it when it was ready for us.

4.08 On Our Own

Shortly after the acquisition, our parent Visual Products Division decided to shed the Industrial Optics project to downsize the staff and improve its profit and loss statement (P&L). As a result, we became a separate department reporting to Ken Schoen, one of the graphic systems group's vice presidents. This actually gave us more freedom to focus on developing the market and business. The project was also becoming a technical resource for a number of the other 3M divisions that began utilizing and needing our technology and expertise:

1. The Traffic Control Products Division was in the process of scaling up the manufacture of cube-corner retroreflective sheeting.
2. The Visual Products Division was expanding its overhead projector line and needed advanced and improved echelon lenses.
3. The Magnetic Products Division was developing information storage systems and required diamond-machining capability to produce precision magnetic hard drives.
4. Other divisions were becoming interested in micro-structured surface technology and wanted research and development access to the technology as well.

All told, there were five separate engineering proposals to develop and expand 3M's diamond-machining technology, capability, and capacity.

4.09 Acquiring Capability

I had developed an eye condition that severely affected my vision. I was referred to Dr. Arthur Jampolsky, an ophthalmologist at the Smith Kettlewell Institute in San Francisco, California, for consultation in treating my condition.

During a conversation with Dr. Jampolsky, I learned that

he had started a company, Optical Sciences Group Inc., to manufacture and distribute echelon ophthalmic correction lenses for treating and correcting vision defects in children. It also produced and marketed a wide angle echelon lens under the name "Vanguard" for use on the rear window of buses and vans that widened the rear field of view for the driver. Recently, it had developed and was manufacturing a large echelon lens for the emerging large-screen projection TV market.

Art indicated he was looking for a buyer of the business. We already had our own echelon lens technology and manufacturing capability, so I told him that we weren't particularly interested. However, I agreed to look into it anyway.

I was in for a surprise. While touring their facility, Art disclosed that they were currently completing the design, development, and construction of a highly advanced diamond-turning machine they called the DTM-4. The development was under the direction and supervision of their employee Bill Bryan in collaboration with Cranfield University in England. Bill's background was in precision machining technology and Cranfield was known for its research and development of advanced micromachining systems and equipment.

The business was relatively small, and its manufacturing capability provided no additional advantage. However, its technical personnel and micromachining development were of great value. When completed, this one machine would meet or exceed all of 3M's micromachining requirements, accelerate the development of our micromachining capability by several years, and eliminate the need to design, engineer, and purchase five different diamond-machining machines. The technical staff was outstanding and possessed the skills we needed for not only our new optical businesses but to support other corporate structured-surface micromachining needs.

Diamond Turning Machine—The DTM-4

We acquired the company. The cost of acquisition was actually less than the estimated cost of the five diamond-machining machines that had been proposed. The acquisition plan was

1. complete the design, construction and instillation of Optical Sciences Group's diamond machining

facility;

2. support our own as well as other corporate developments in structured surface technology; and

3. ensure that the Optical Sciences Group's technical staff would be retained and assimilated into 3M.

4.10 Organizing for Growth

Following the acquisition of Optical Sciences Group, our Industrial Optics business was still struggling. There were numerous customers, but most were low-volume or short-term applications. Rear-projection screens had sales volume, but profitability was low due to competition. We had optical technology that the electronic display markets would eventually need, but we were technically ahead of that market by several years. In addition, the internal demand for our optical design, structured surface development, and micromachining services was growing and absorbing most if not all of our technical personnel and expertise. But that didn't pay the bills or help grow our Industrial Optics business.

It became obvious that serving as a corporate technical resource and developing a new business at the same time wasn't going to work. Our group met, discussed the problem, and concluded that the only practical solution was to divide the project into two separate groups:

1. The first group would become a corporate resource or technical center, which would support the business units that were developing products utilizing the technology and promote

microreplication technology throughout the company.

2. The second group would be the original Industrial Optics business unit, which would rely upon support from the technical center for product development, manufacturing scale up, etc.

Creating a technology center that would focus on a specific technology platform was a new concept at 3M. What to call it was a problem. The technology was being referred to as microreplication. However, the upper management became concerned that using that name might be too descriptive and prematurely broadcast our technological strategy. We settled on naming it the "Optics Technology Center."

The significant change in organization that we proposed required corporate approval. The company was divided into several sectors with the Industrial Optics Department reporting to the Life Sciences Sector. Our sector R&D vice president, Ron Mitsch, said I had five minutes to present the proposal at the corporate review. I never worked so hard preparing a five-minute presentation in my life! Explaining the technology-center concept and how it would function was a challenge, particularly when most of the upper management knew little about the technology or its opportunities.

In my five-minute presentation, I explained what the structured surface technology was, demonstrated examples of the technology, which spanned the corporate divisions and sectors, and outlined the technology that had to be developed. Those developments included the following:

1. Expanding structured surface design
2. Development of advanced diamond cutting tools
3. Scale up of precision micromachining, (i.e., diamond turning)
4. Development of structured surface micro metrology
5. Development of structured surface tooling substrates and replication technology
6. Identification and development of molding materials suitable for the replication of structured surfaces
7. Development of a continuous microreplication manufacturing process

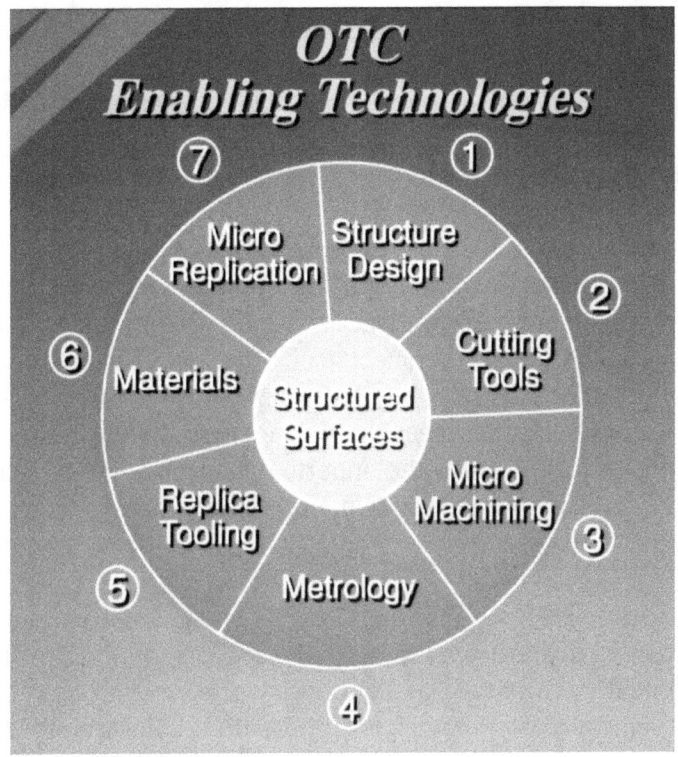

Microreplication-Enabling Technologies

The presentation was exactly five minutes long and the proposal was approved. After the review, Ron Mitsch said he had never seen a corporate proposal presented and approved in just five minutes, and that he wouldn't have objected if I had taken a little more time.

4.11 Top-Down Education and Promotion

After the approval to create the Optics Technology Center, we ended up with a laboratory in Petaluma,

California, a development facility in Menomonee, Wisconsin, and several separate laboratories at the 3M research campus near Saint Paul, Minnesota. With laboratories in so many different locations, I needed to decide in which laboratory my office would be located.

After considerable thought, I decided to locate it near the corporate administrative office complex rather than in one of the laboratories. Not having an office in one of the labs made little difference since I had to visit and work with all the labs on a regular basis anyway. However, by locating my office near the management of the business divisions, it afforded the opportunity for me and my staff to interface with the upper management on almost a daily basis.

Informing or promoting management with a new innovative idea, technology, or product opportunity has typically followed a bottom-up process through the organization with management usually the last to see and approve it. This is a serial approach, where each level in the organization incorporates their product concepts before it is approved and passed onto the next level. When it formally reaches upper management, the management team tends to be more skeptical since it had received the least amount of knowledge and exposure to the development.

However, having my office in the administrative building gave us the opportunity to interface with management in the hallway, at special events, or frequently for lunch, and presell its members on new technologies and ideas during the earliest stages of development. If we had a new innovative idea and particularly if we had produced a sample, I would make sure we ran into the management that might have a business interest in it. This was a "top-down" education process during the earliest stages of a development that kept management informed of the technology, its progress, and the potential opportunity. It also gave us valuable insight into its thinking, which helped guide the development. This approach worked very well and became our "management show-and-tell" strategy.

As an example, the lab had made some experimental samples of a structured-surface abrasive film designed by Gary Holms that had surprising and unexpected abrasive properties. It was sandpaper without sand! One day, I joined John Friswold, general manager of the Automotive Products Division, and Dick McGrath, vice president of the Abrasive Products Division, for lunch. I reached into my pocket and showed them a sample of the structured surface material and demonstrated how well it functioned as an abrasive. Soon, we were discussing how this might revolutionize the abrasive technology, products, and business. That lunch changed the attitude of management from that of being "skeptical" to being a "champion" for the new technology. It sparked a major product scale-up project to produce and market it. Today, that product is known as the "3M Trizact Abrasive" product line, which played a major role in reinventing and revitalizing the original and oldest 3M business, the 3M Abrasive Products Division.

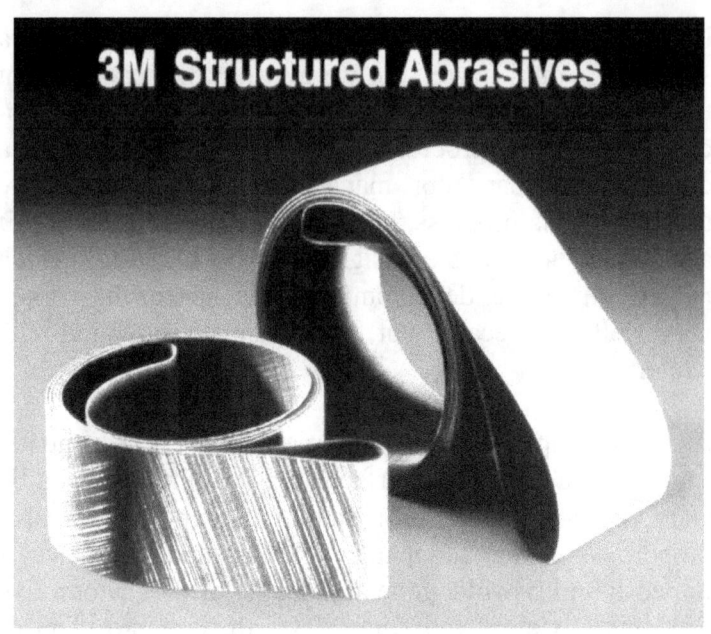

3M Trizact Structured-Surface Abrasives

On another occasion, we demonstrated a microstructured film that would spread or transport a fluid in one direction to Jack Zoia, general manager of the Diaper Products Division. That got him thinking about its possible use in diapers and incontinence pads to more evenly distribute the fluid so that the absorbent pad or diaper could be made thinner and more comfortable. He became a strong champion, overseeing the development and incorporation of the technology into its products.

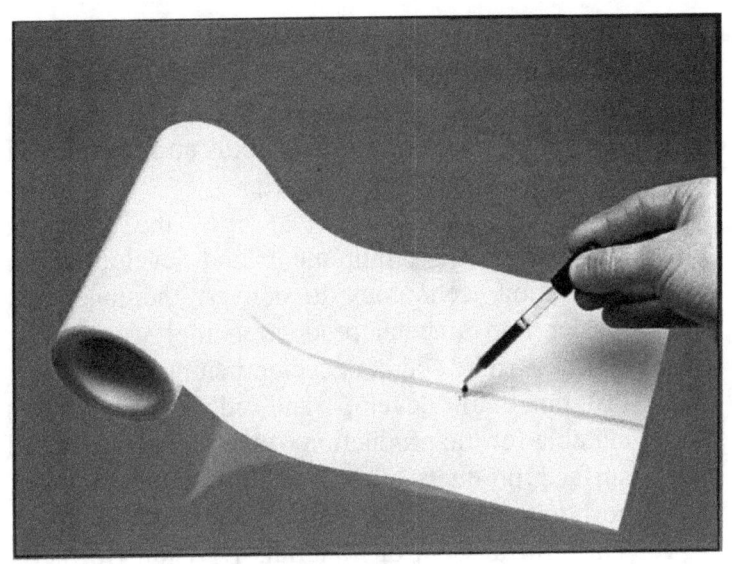

Fluid Transfer Film

4.12 The Enabling Technologies

With the establishment of the Optics Technology Center, development of the essential enabling technologies as proposed to corporate management began in earnest:

1. Combining the Optical Science Group personnel with our own staff created an outstanding structured-surface design and development team.
2. A cutting-tool laboratory under the direction of Gary Lundgren to design, develop, and manufacture our own diamond cutting tools was created to ensure tool quality and reliability.
3. The new high-precision micromachining facility acquired through the acquisition of Optical Sciences Group provided an advanced world-

leading precision micromachining capability known as the "DTM-4."

4. Micrometrology instruments for inspecting and measuring structured surface tools and the molded replicas were being developed.

5. Developing substrates that met the exacting micromachining requirements and developing the replication technology to convert the machined master into a metal production tool was led by Harlan Krinke and his development team.

6. Programs to develop and identify polymers suitable for the production of the varied structured surface products were established within other corporate materials and process laboratories.

7. The Traffic Control Materials Division (formerly the Reflective Products Division) was developing a structured-surface continuous molding process to produce cube-corner retroreflective sheeting led by Tim Hoopman.

We were now on our way toward establishing a new corporate technology platform that would serve the entire company by creating a multitude of new products and businesses, a platform that came to be known as "microreplication."

However, the development and scale-up of a continuous replication process proved to be one of the most difficult and challenging technical hurdles. Replicating a structured surface pattern in a polymer one at a time was one thing, but a continuous process that would hold tolerances measured in wave lengths of light or even nanometers in the replicated structure over the life of the product is another thing. Thermal, mechanical, physical, and chemical constraints dominated every aspect of the process, beginning with the process equipment all the way through to the final product.

After numerous attempts using different process equipment designs and a variety of replicating polymers, satisfactory replication of the microstructure topography on the tool was not being achieved. In an attempt to find a set of parameters where successful replication could be achieved, comprehensive design experiments were performed where the process variables were systematically varied within their known physical and chemical limits. Unfortunately, no set of process parameters where a complete and stable replication of the structure could be achieved was found.

This was a tremendous setback not only to the development of cube-corner retroreflective sheeting development but to the development of structured-surface microreplication as a whole. Sadly, a review meeting needed to be scheduled with the top corporate management to inform it of the problem. The meeting was to take place at our manufacturing development facility in Wisconsin. At stake was the very survival of the program.

As preparations were being made for the meeting, and as we were literally waiting for management to arrive, it was decided that we would run one more test where some of the process parameters would be extended into what had been defined as "forbidden regions." 3M polymer experts had warned that in doing so, the stability and durability of the product would be compromised and lost. We ran the test anyway. Amazingly, it worked, and there appeared to be no degradation to the final product at all!

A management review that had threatened to terminate further development turned into a meeting of cautious celebration and management approval to continue the development and scale up, *if* in fact it was proven that there had been no degradation to the product. Further tests confirmed there had been no degradation.

The Traffic Control Materials Division cautiously proceeded with the development of the continuous replication process for manufacturing cube-corner retroreflective sheeting. The division wasn't convinced that there was a substantial market for a new retroreflective product, even if it did have superior brightness and performance over beaded sheeting. It had concluded that the product would probably be limited to specialty applications such as retroreflective truck markings or what was known as "truck conspicuity," for example. In addition, skepticism was growing among some sectors and corporate management about the wisdom of investing in the development of microreplication technology. It became obvious that we needed to demonstrate the utility and value of microreplication process—and soon.

Sandia Laboratories in Albuquerque, New Mexico, was evaluating and testing echelon lenses for solar photovoltaic concentrators and had issued a request for bids to demonstrate the feasibility of manufacturing large arrays of high-quality echelon or Fresnel lenses. This was an opportunity to demonstrate our microreplication technology and capability. Paul Jaster, a corporate engineer assigned to the Optics Technology Center, wrote and submitted a proposal to Sandia Laboratories to manufacture and deliver within a year several rolls of echelon lens arrays one meter wide and several hundred meters in length for a specified fee. Sandia approved the proposal, and we went to work.

The production of the lens arrays helped accelerate and defray the cost of the microreplication facility and demonstrate its structured-surface production capability. The rolls of lens film produced were very impressive. The lenses met and exceeded all the optical performance requirements and looked like crystal.

Solar Energy Concentrating Lens Film

Before we delivered the rolls of lenses to Sandia, we scheduled a luncheon and invited key sector and corporate management to see the new lens-film product. The tables were arranged in a triangle around the rolls of lens film we had just produced so everyone could see them. Our sector vice president, Livio DeSimone, better known as Desi, attended the luncheon and became enthralled with the crystalline-like rolls of lens film. Desi asked many questions and kept getting up to look at and feel the lens film. For Desi, microreplication was suddenly a reality that represented a substantial new business potential for 3M. Desi never did finish his lunch.

The result of that luncheon meeting was a number of corporate managers and vice presidents, including Desi, becoming enthusiastic champions of the microreplication technology and its many potential uses and new business opportunities.

The Traffic Control Materials Division introduced the new cube-corner retroreflective product two years later as 3M Diamond Grade Reflective Sheeting. It was an immediate success, exceeding all expectations. It not only became the standard retroreflective marking material for the truck conspicuity application, but it was soon replacing the retroreflective sheeting on nearly all signs—worldwide.

4.13 Acquiring Innovation and Technology

At about the same time that we were working with the Sandia Labs to produce an echelon lens film, Sandy Cobb was researching the optical properties of a unique prismatic optical film. The film had a series of linear prisms on one surface, the faces of which were disposed at angles of ninety degrees with respect to one another. Due to the orientation of the prism faces, the film was capable of totally reflecting light entering the film on the smooth side. If, for example, the film was rolled into a tube with the prisms on the outside and parallel to the length of the tube, light entering the tube from one end would be totally reflected by the film prisms, and the light would be conducted or piped down through the tube. This created a light pipe.

One of the opportunities we had identified for optical structured surfaces was light management, which included lighting or illumination applications. Pursuing our interest in lighting applications and the unique properties of the prismatic film, Sandy attended a lighting conference in Arizona. There he met Dr. Loren Whitehead from Vancouver, British Colombia, who gave a talk on the development of a light-pipe lighting fixture he had invented that was able to conduct and distribute light over long distances from a single or compact light source.

Loren had formed a company, TIR Inc., to manufacture and market the technology. The light-pipe product he invented used rigid molded transparent panels with the large ninety-degree linear prisms molded on one side. The panels were assembled into a square tube with a single compact light source located at one end. A strip of light-diffusing material was placed within the tube following the length of the pipe, which scattered a portion of the light, allowing it to leak out the side of the tube.

The result was a light fixture that evenly distributed light from a single light source over distances of many feet.

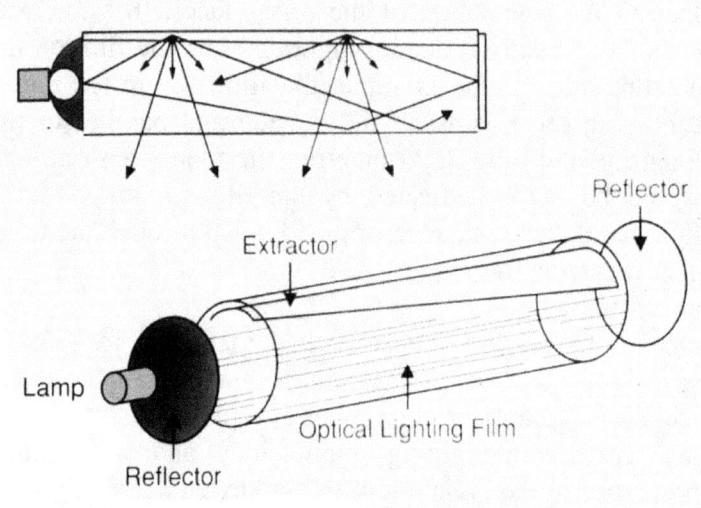

TIR Light-Pipe Light Fixture

Sandy introduced himself to Loren and mentioned that 3M had developed a TIR (Total Internal Reflection) film. He suggested that 3M might be interested in producing the thin, flexible, prismatic film as an alternative to the molded panels he was making. Loren said he was interested, so we invited Dr. Whitehead to visit 3M to present his technology, product developments, and business plan.

As a result of that visit, a fruitful relationship was established between Loren and 3M. 3M agreed to produce the flexible prismatic film for Loren and 3M would license Whitehead's patents and technology. In addition, 3M would initiate a lighting project and work with Loren to jointly develop lighting products and applications using the TIR technology. The production of TIR film on the Traffic Control Materials Division microreplication facility was successful, and we began supplying film to Loren and to our own lighting project. A variety of applications for the light pipe lighting was soon found, including accent lighting on buildings, hallway lighting, guiderail illumination on roadways, safety lighting, and more.

In this day of high-speed computers that are literally at our fingertips, complex mathematical modeling and analysis has not only become commonplace, it has become a standard or primary tool in the research and development process. Complex problems with many variables can be modeled on the computer to determine their effects and quickly modified until desired results are obtained, all without leaving one's desk. Failed parameters and results are simply discarded and forgotten.

A significant innovative idea is frequently the result of observing and pursing an unplanned, failed, or unexpected result. Unfortunately, many, if not most, of these observations are obscured or never noticed with computer modeling. Although the computer is an indispensable tool, it is also essential to regularly work with the real thing in the real world away from the computer. I have always advocated turning off the computer, at least one day a week for example, getting away from your desk, talking with real people, and working with and observing the new things you are working on. In other words, spend a day at the lab bench.

As an example, one day we were examining (playing) with the new TIR film in the laboratory and admiring its visual properties and effects, many of which, if not all, are not visible, nor can they be appreciated in the computer models of the film. This film had an unexpected surprise in store for us that later proved to be a major game changer.

Laying the TIR film on a diffuse light source with the smooth side against the light source, we were astonished to observe that it actually increased the brightness of the light source—I couldn't believe it! One of the principles taught in physical optics is that the brightness of a diffuse or lambertian source of light cannot be increased with an optical lens or concentrator. For example, the surface of the sun is a lambertian light source. The brightness of an image of the sun formed by an optical element, such as a lens, cannot exceed the brightness of the surface of the sun. But there I was, looking at diffuse light source that was clearly brighter than it was without the film!

Further testing confirmed that the TIR film did increase the "apparent brightness" of the source. Optical analysis demonstrated that a relatively complex process was at work that directed light traveling more parallel to the surface of the diffuse light source to being more perpendicular or normal to the surface. In other words, the source appeared brighter when viewed from the front and dimmer when viewed at large angles.

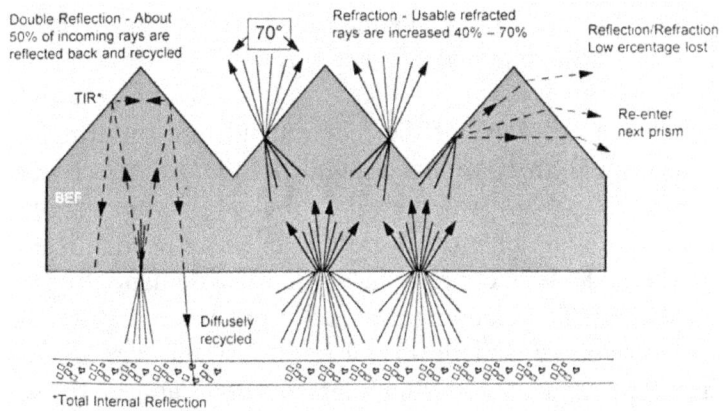

Double Reflection - About 50% of incoming rays are reflected back and recycled

70°

Refraction - Usable refracted rays are increased 40% – 70%

Reflection/Refraction Low ercentage lost

TIR*

BEF

Re-enter next prism

Diffusely recycled

*Total Internal Reflection

TIR Brightness-Enhancement Film Optics

Although the film did increase the apparent brightness of a diffuse light source by a factor of approximately two, it didn't appear that much brighter to the eye. At the time it was easier and, we thought, cheaper to just turn up the brightness of the light source than add the cost of the TIR film. As a result, this new discovery remained on the shelf (but was not forgotten) for the time being.

4.14 Bumps in the Road

All this while, the Industrial Optics department was still struggling to build a profitable business. The major market for rear-projection screens was rapidly shrinking. Computers with CRT (cathode ray tube) displays were replacing microfilm readers and printers. We decided to sell the optical screen business to the Da-Lite company located in Warsaw, Indiana. There were customers for the other optical products, but the volume wasn't there yet. Some of the members of 3M management became discouraged and recommended that the Industrial Optics business be terminated.

When we got wind of the recommendation to terminate Industrial Optics, we just couldn't let that happen. I went to see Desi, who was now the CEO of 3M, and argued that significant changes were taking place in the display market that would create a substantial demand for our structured film technologies and products. For example, the development of flat-panel liquid-crystal displays had made portable laptop computers feasible, and there was every indication that the liquid-crystal displays would soon replace the CRT not only in computers but in TV systems as well. Liquid-crystal displays would need our optical-film technologies to improve their performance and acceptance. Further, the market for optical films would be enormous. Laptop computers alone could consume many millions of square feet of optical film annually. I don't know how much influence I had with Desi, but in any event, the Industrial Optics business was given a reprieve.

Industrial Optics wasn't the only thing that was on the chopping block.

As I write this, I may leave the impression that there were no disagreements, that all things proceeded smoothly, and that there weren't any confrontations. That's not true, and one must recognize that no matter how hard you try, not everyone will always agree with your ideas or support you. I ran into my share of bumps in the road as well.

A change in management or management attitude,

economic conditions, business conditions, etc., can threaten your career and all you have worked for. Most organizations, particularly businesses and corporations, by their nature or by necessity are not benevolent, democratic institutions. They can be autocratic, dictatorial, political, and capricious.

About a year after the introduction of Diamond Grade Sheeting, there was a change in management, and we ended up with a new vice president, who I'll refer to here as "VP." VP didn't share our vision and had opposed 3M's investment in the microreplication technology. On one occasion, he said that microreplication was a low-level technology not worthy of investment. He ordered that I be removed from my position and offered me an undefined management position in Japan, which would completely remove me from any further involvement with the microreplication technology and the Optics Technology Center.

I was warned that no one at 3M had ever turned down an overseas assignment. I consulted with the "champions" I had cultivated at 3M, and they all advised that I refuse the offer. After a long discussion with my wife, Marilyn, and my family, and knowing that I might lose my job, I told VP that I would not accept his offer.

After some further turmoil and to make a long story short, Dave Sonstegard, my immediate manager, promoted me to the position of corporate scientist, the highest technical position in the company. This permitted me to continue interfacing with and promoting the technology, the laboratories, and the business units. Most importantly, the

Optics Technology Center and the new product development programs would remain intact.

I never understood why the VP was so negative. There are many possible explanations not worth pursuing or thinking about. However, the most important lesson I learned was how important it is to cultivate as many champions as possible. I'm certain that without their support and influence, I wouldn't be writing this story.

4.15 The Market Catches Up

With the development of the laptop computer, a number of technical advancements were needed to make it more portable and practical. Laptop computers require rechargeable batteries to power the computers and light the displays. Liquid-crystal displays needed to be backlit with lamps that consumed most of the battery power. The tradeoffs were

1. a brighter display but shorter battery life;
2. a longer battery life but a dimmer display; or
3. a bright display with a bigger, heavier, and more expensive battery for longer life.

The computer industry turned toward investing in developing brighter light sources and more powerful—but more expensive—battery technology.

Recognizing the computer industry's need for bright displays and a long battery life, Sandy Cobb, Terry Jones, Olester Benson, and others dusted off the TIR brightness enhancement technology that we had discovered and put on the shelf earlier. The tradeoffs it potentially offered the computer industry were

1. a display that was twice as bright using the existing battery;
2. a display with the same brightness but with a battery half the size; or
3. a display with the same brightness and battery but with twice the life.

Even if a more efficient battery was developed, a less expensive, smaller battery or longer battery life would always be possible with the use of the TIR technology.

At this point, it was essential that we protect the TIR brightness-enhancement discovery with patents. Surprisingly, our patent attorney, Steve Buckingham, discovered that Dr. Loren Whitehead had also observed the brightness-enhancement effect and had included it in the claims of one of his patents that 3M had licensed. A fortuitous display of serendipity.

Industrial Optics reengineered the TIR film for use on optical displays and named it 3M Brightness Enhancement Film, or BEF. With samples of BEF in hand, Terry Jones headed to Japan to demonstrate and sell the product to the computer industry. Toshiba became the first customer and soon all the other manufactures began to follow suit.

4.16 Innovation Continues

The 3M Film Division had been developing an extrusion

process to extrude a stack of many thin films into a single multilayer film to improve physical and mechanical properties. Dow had been developing a similar process and had produced multilayer films composed of a stack of thin films with alternating optical properties. One of their developments was a multilayer film that was highly reflective to light without the need for metallic or other reflective coatings.

Dow lost interest, however, and offered to sell their technology to 3M. After the acquisition of their technology, Ron Tabor of the 3M Film Division and I coordinated the transfer of the Du Pont technology and organized a 3M research and development program to further explore and develop the technology. The overall objective was to develop multilayer films that had unique physical, mechanical, and optical properties.

Multiple thin layers of optical film was another form of incremental optics that offered new opportunities in light management and control. We envisioned films with unique optical properties, including optical color filters, specialized reflective films, and polarizing films, to name a few.

Extruding a multilayer film only a few thousandths of an inch thick, consisting of many hundreds of microthin layers of film, was a challenge, to say the least. Even more daunting was producing multilayer films that had uniform optical properties over large areas. Many believed it to be an expensive gamble if not an impossible task.

However, Andy Ouderkirk, Terrence Neavin, Michael Weber, James Jonza, Carl Stover, and others did not believe it was impossible and accepted the challenge. They not only perfected the processes but made major innovative optical advances and inventions as well. They developed films with 100 percent reflectivity, transmissive or reflective color filter films, and a revolutionary reflection polarizer.

A liquid-crystal display requires polarized light for the liquid crystal to function as a light valve or switch. Conventional polarizers such as dichroic polymer films transmit light that is polarized along the polarizing axis of the film and absorb light that is at right angles to the polarizing axis. As a result, 50 percent of the light is lost forever to absorption.

The 3M multilayer polarizer functions in the same way, but it reflects the light at right angles to the axis of the film back toward the light source rather than absorbing it. The reflected light can then be recycled and polarized as well, effectively doubling the brightness of a display that had used conventional polarizers. Combined with the microstructured brightness-enhancement film, the composite structure almost quadruples the efficiency and brightness of a liquid-crystal display.

Liquid-crystal display devices could now be thinner, lighter, have longer battery lives, and consume less energy.

4.17 Postscripts

By 1995, a host of microreplication and optics products and new business units had become or were becoming a reality. Examples include the following:

1. 3M overhead projectors
2. Optically programmable traffic signals
3. High-performance Diamond-Grade retroreflective sheeting for highway signs
4. Solar concentrating and energy films
5. Brightness-enhancement films for optical displays (computers, cell phones, TVs, etc.)
6. Reflection polarizers for liquid-crystal displays
7. Sandpaper with no sand (3M Trizact Abrasives)
8. Fluid-transport control film
9. Transdermal drug delivery film
10. Bubble-free adhesive films
11. Lighting and energy control products

In 1995, the stock analysts were scheduled to review and evaluate 3M businesses and business plans. Desi asked that I review 3M's products, businesses, and business plans related to the microreplication investment.

At past reviews, the stock analysts had always been interested in 3M's investments in innovative new technologies, products, and the new business opportunities they represented. We would take them on tours through the laboratories and demonstrate some of the numerous new technologies and innovative products for which they gave 3M high marks.

At this review, however, the analysts expressed little to no interest in microreplication or our new product developments. They questioned our investment and were more concerned about how the investment would affect current earnings than how it would create new business growth opportunities. When they asked what our sales and financial projections were, I reported that in 1993 we had analyzed the business opportunity and had concluded potential annual sales would be in the $3.6 billion range within the next eight to ten years. They laughed, berated me, and suggested that corporate scientists don't have the credentials, skills, or knowledge to make such wild and unfounded predictions.

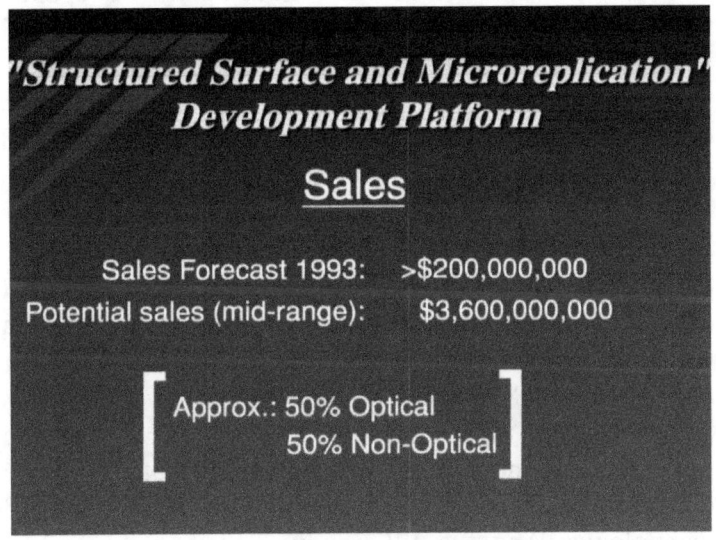

**1993 Opportunity Analysis Forecast for
Microreplication**

I retired in 1996 but continued on as a consultant at 3M for another ten years.

A year following my retirement in 1996, I attended a retirement party for Tom Reed, a renowned corporate scientist. The vice president who had not supported the microreplication program was there also. During the party, Desi announced that the Optical Systems Department, formerly Industrial Optics, was experiencing phenomenal sales growth and profits and would soon be named a division. VP didn't apologize, but he looked at me, shook his head, and said, "And to think we almost shut the whole thing down."

In 2005, the *3M Stemwinder*, a company newspaper, reported that the display and graphics businesses' 2004 sales were $3.2 billion with operating income totaling $1.1 billion. The bulk of these sales were based upon optical microreplication technology and products. We had the last laugh over the analysts after all!

In September of 2012, Fred Polanski, senior vice president of Research and Development, announced that annual sales of products based upon microreplication technology accounted for 35 percent of 3M sales or approximately $11 billion annually, all of which can traced back to the development of the 3M overhead projector and the process of innovation that led to the creation of the microreplication family of innovations and technologies. And it is still growing...

The Display and Graphics Business, formed in 2002, is a technology innovator and market leader globally. But first and foremost, it's a growth engine.

Consider these numbers. Sales rose 11.5 percent in 2002, 33.0 percent (about 22 percent excluding acquisitions) in 2003 and 15.0 percent in 2004. Profits increased 43.5 percent in 2002, 65.8 percent in 2003 and 27.8 percent in 2004.

In 2004, sales reached $3.4 billion and operating income totaled $1.1 billion. Operating income was 33.2 percent of sales, up from 18.6 percent in 2001.

Behind these numbers are four hard-working divisions — Optical Systems, Traffic Safety Systems, Commercial Graphics, and Specialty Film and Media Products — that are focused on driving profitable growth.

"This is a fantastic set of businesses, with outstanding technology, strong relationships with customers, leading market positions, and talented and dedicated people," said Jim Stake, executive vice president, Display and Graphics Business.

Optical Systems

Optical Systems is one of 3M's largest and fastest-growing businesses. This division is home to Vikuiti™ Display Enhancement Films, which make electronic displays brighter, more colorful and easier to read.

"Our films are sold to virtually every major liquid crystal display [LCD] screen manufacturer in the world today," Stake said. "This is an outstanding growth industry and will continue to be for years to come."

Excerpt from the *3M Stemwinder*, March–April, 2005

5.00 Fifteen Principles of the Innovation Process

1. **Encourage and Exercise Initiative: 2.01**
    "The Challenge of Management" by William McKnight
2. **15 Percent Rule: 3.02, 4.02**
    Devote 15 percent of your working hours on your own independent innovative projects.
3. **Opportunity Analysis: 3.03, 4.05, 4.06, 4.07**
    Define, quantify, and model the value of an opportunity at the earliest stages.
4. **Make-a-Little, Sell-a-Little**: **3.02**
    Sell and test the innovation in the real world with real customers as early as possible.
5. **Vision: 3.02, 3.05, 4.07**
    Develop a clear and detailed picture of the desired end result or objective.
6. **Encourage Everyone to Be Innovative: 3.08**
    Encourage everyone to overcome their inhibitions to innovate.
7. **Wants vs. Needs: 3.07, 4.15**
    Define what the customers' real "needs" are beyond their stated "wants."
8. **Focus on the New and Unexpected: 4.02, 4.13**
    Look for and pursue new-to-the-world innovative ideas and opportunities.
9. **Financial Modeling: 4.06, 4.07**
    Create financial models (i.e., pro forma profit-and-loss statements), of the new opportunity and business.
10. **Innovation Planning: 4.12**
    Identify the enabling technologies needed for success.

11. **Acquire Supporting Innovations and Technology Whenever Possible: 4.09, 4.13, 4.16**
Acquire enabling technology whenever possible. Don't reinvent the wheel!

12. **Multitasking and Technical Diversity: 4.05, 4.09, 4.13**
Successful innovation requires many different skills and capabilities. No new idea or product is a singular innovation but is the assembly of many.

13. **Overcome Obstacles: 3.07**
Innovate ways around restrictive or unnecessary rules and procedures.

14. **Cultivate Champions: 3.01, 4.02**
Develop relationships with those who understand and share your vision.

15. **Top-Down Promotion and Selling: 4.11**
Educate management about new opportunities as they evolve and as early as possible. Reduce or eliminate perceived risk with knowledge and education.

People are the most important factor in the innovation process. William McKnight recognized this in his letter to management when he focused on encouraging men and women to exercise their innovative initiative. People tend to shy away from exercising their innovative talent due to the social or cultural inhibitions they grew up with or were taught. My most gratifying experiences have been encouraging and helping people overcome their inhibitions and become productive innovators.

Various programs, methods, and procedures have been developed to guide and manage existing and new businesses. They all have their place and many have proven their value when properly applied. However, most, if not all, are sequential or step-by-step methods that focus on substantially reducing, if not eliminating, the chance of a mistake or failure.

In the 1950s, a program known as "The Critical Path Method" became popular. It tracked a development program through its <u>sequential</u> activities from the start to the end of the project. In the 1980s, a quality improvement program titled "Six Sigma" was developed by Motorola. It is described as a <u>step-by-step process</u> that helps a company or organization focus on developing and delivering products and services that are nearly flawless. (The Six Sigma standard strove for processes, products, services, etc., with no more than 3.4 defects or errors per million.) In programs like these, emphasis is on low-risk, known, and familiar approaches or technologies with a strong tendency to avoid or reject unfamiliar or new innovative ideas perceived to be high risk. However, as McKnight pointed out, being destructively critical of new ideas can kill initiative and growth.

The Innovation Process

1. The innovation process is driven by an individual or team referred to as an "innoventorpreneure." (See section 8.06)
2. This innoventorpreneure remains intimately involved through all phases of the innovation process.
3. The innovation process may be best characterized as a parallel process where all functions interact,

collaborate, and work together throughout the program toward common innovative goals and objectives from beginning to introduction and beyond.

4. It begins with the interaction, involvement and understanding of the user or customer's business, needs, and expectations.

5. Its focus is on meeting or exceeding the users' or customers' needs and expectations.

6. Exorcizing innovative initiative is encouraged and promoted throughout the organization.

7. It is a flexible discovery process that continuously updates, modifies, and adapts as new innovative discoveries or contributions are developed. It may even alter or change the original objectives or direction of the project. (Looking back over the numerous developments and products related to incremental optics, structured surfaces and microreplication technologies, many were unplanned, unexpected, or even accidental.)

8. Successful high-value innovative products, programs, and businesses are the assembly of multiple innovative ideas and developments at all stages and levels of the program—not just one.

6.00 The Need to Innovate

6.01 The Decline of US Innovation

Around twenty-five to thirty years ago, innovation, particularly in the United States, began to decline. Lew Lehr, the CEO of 3M, could see it coming as early as 1980. He recognized that a number of changes in the business and economic climate were taking place that could threaten the 3M culture of innovation and ultimately the growth of 3M. Some of the changes he outlined to us were

1. uncertainty in the availability and cost of supplies and raw materials;
2. changes in the corporate tax structure;
3. acquisitions viewed as an alternative to innovation; and
4. focus on maximizing short-term financial returns at the expense of long-term investment.

Lew called a meeting that included Julie Prager, director of Corporate Planning, and Les Krogh, vice president of Research and Development, and asked that we develop plans and programs to promote and maintain innovation within 3M to ensure that 3M would never lose this unique culture. In response, several corporate programs were implemented:

1. **Employee innovation courses**—to acquaint and educate technical employees with the 3M Innovation Process culture
2. **Mentoring**—3M corporate scientists established

conferences and programs to mentor rising innovative employees.

3. **Management Innovation Seminars**—to assist management in creating and maintaining a climate and culture for innovation.

As a result, innovation is still alive and well at 3M. However, the changes Lew recognized did happen, and innovation did suffer—nationwide. This has negatively impacted growth, jobs, personal income, etc. The following are a few examples.

6.02 Maximizing Return

On several occasions, I was asked to arrange a tour for the stock analysts through some of our laboratories and demonstrate the new technologies and products that 3M was investing in. This was an exciting highlight for the analysts and they gave 3M high marks for its innovative developments and investments. However, that was about to change.

As I mentioned in section 4.16, in 1996, Desi asked that I review 3M's investment in microreplication technologies and its related products for the stock analysts that year. Surprisingly, the analysts showed little interest in the technology or the new products. Instead, they questioned 3M's wisdom in making the investment and warned that the expense would negatively affect 3M's return. I responded that 3M expected annual sales of microreplication products to exceed $3.6 billion within the next eight to ten years. They laughed, saying the estimate wasn't realistic and questioned my authority to make such predictions. However, eight years later, in 2004, 3M reported that sales of microreplication products had exceeded $3 billion annually. We had the last laugh.

6.03 Downsizing

Overall, however, the industry-wide business strategy to maximize return at the expense of investing in innovation drove outsourcing and downsizing strategies.

In 1996, 3M also followed the corporate-wide strategy of downsizing through early retirements and layoffs. I estimate that more than ten thousand 3M technical employees were let go, many of whom were 3M's most experienced innovators. Virtually every Fortune 500 corporation in the United States followed this strategy and was cheered on, if not directed to do so, by Wall Street.

Nationwide, well over five million of our most innovative people had been "deactivated." Not only were their innovative skills shelved, they were no longer available to mentor the remaining and new employees. Where did all these innovators go? One might expect they would have used their innovative skills to create a surge in business startups, but that has not happened. In fact, just the opposite has occurred largely due to post-retirement restrictions imposed on them and the lack of resources and capital.

In addition, downsizing brought hiring to all but a halt, severely limiting new employment opportunities.

6.04 Acquisitions and Mergers vs. Innovation

Acquisitions and mergers also preempted innovation investments throughout the United States. Many innovative companies have disappeared under the pressures of corporate raiders and mergers. Historically, 3M's growth has been internally generated through the development of new products and businesses. Acquisitions made in the past generally provided needed technologies or increased capabilities. However, in 2005, 3M implemented an aggressive acquisition strategy. Between 2005 and 2011, seventy-seven acquisitions were made to bolster sales and returns.

A more detailed study and analysis of the decline of "creativity" in the United States is analyzed by Thomas L. Friedman and Michael Mandelbaum in their book, *That Used to Be Us: How America Fell Behind in the World It Invented and How We Can Come Back.*

7.00 Innovation, a New Opportunity

7.01 The Emerging Need for Innovation and Innovators

In their book *That Used to Be US**, Friedman and Mandelbaum point to four key challenges that face our nation:

1. The IT revolution
2. Deficits and debt
3. Energy
4. The environment

Although we face these serious challenges and problems, I believe they also represent substantial opportunities.

The IT revolution is still evolving, and we have hardly learned to crawl with it. Much has to be done to adapt it to our requirements, needs, and uses.

Deficits and debt can be best dealt with by growing our economy. One could argue that the deficits are linked to the decline of innovation. Innovation is the key to growing industry, jobs, the economy, and leadership in the world. A growing economy pays the bills.

Energy is a critical global issue and must be dealt with. Renewable and alternative energy systems are on the verge of outpacing fossil fuels and driving a host of new

---

* Thomas L. Friedman and Michael Mandelbaum: *That Used to BE US, How America Fell Behind In The World It Invented and How We Can Come Back* (Farrar, Straus and Ciroux 2011)

innovative industries. For example, technology that significantly reduces the energy requirements of our devices, manufacturing systems, transportation, etc., is just around the corner and is waiting to be developed and implemented.

The environment sustains all of us. If we don't sustain it, it will not sustain us. Regardless of the cause, literally thousands of scientists are telling us (if not yelling at us!) that we have a really big climate problem on our hands—*right now*! The solution to these environmental and climate problems will take all the technology and innovative skills we can muster.

7.02 3M Leading in Innovation—Again

In the fall of 2013, 3M announced a $150 to $200 million investment in new and expanded research facilities here in Minnesota. This investment ensures that the hub of 3M research and innovation will remain and grow in Minnesota. In addition, 3M CEO, Inge Thulin, announced that 3M would increase its $1.63 billion research and development investment with an increased focus on developing "new-to-the-world innovative technologies and businesses."

7.03 The Need for Innovators

If I am just partially correct, there will be a growing demand for innovators—in all fields. But where will these innovators be found? I know of no school, college, or university that offers courses or prepares students in the skills of innovation. In their book, *That Used to Be*

Us, Friedman and Mandelbaum call for the following:

Teaching and inspiring creativity. There is no one way to do this and the different attempts to teach creativity (innovation) are among the most exciting experiments in education today. But we know it can be done because other people are doing it.

When Friedman and Mandelbaum use the term "creativity," they are really talking about "innovation." Creativity is one of the skills needed for successful innovation. These skills include

1. creating/inventing;
2. multidisciplinary interest and awareness;
3. financial modeling and analysis;
4. organizational skills;
5. situation analysis and modeling; and
6. listening.

These skills can be taught. 3M has taught them. I have helped teach them! Learning to innovate involves not only learning the basic principles, skills, and techniques, but also learning through association with accomplished innovators.

7.04 Teaching Innovation—At Hamline University

Hamline has the good fortune to have the world's premiere innovative corporation in its backyard. In that backyard there are also the 3M corporate scientists, Carlton Society members, and other special groups that are the recognized experts and leaders in innovation.

Many are willing to share their innovative skills and experiences.

For the thirteenth consecutive year, Hamline University remains the top-ranked Minnesota university in its class.

As I said, I know of no school, college, or university that offers courses or prepares students in the skills of innovation today. Why not be the first college in the state, if not the country, to teach innovation? And to all the Hamline students, I encourage you to innovate your own future by taking every opportunity to learn and practice the skills of the innovation process.

8.00 Exploring the Innovation Process

To review, some of the practices, policies, and techniques that drove and still drive the 3M Innovation Process include the following:

1. Encourage and Exercise Initiative (William McKnight directive)
2. 15 Percent Rule
3. Opportunity Analysis
4. Make-a-Little, Sell-a-Little
5. Vision
6. Encouraging Everyone to Be Innovative
7. Wants vs. Needs
8. Focus on the New
9. Financial Modeling
10. Innovation Planning
11. Acquire Supporting Innovations and Technology When Available
12. Multitasking and Technical Diversity

13. Overcome Obstacles
14. Cultivate Champions
15. Top-Down Promotion and Selling

8.01 What Is Invention?

Invention: An invention is the act of creating a new idea, usually a device or process, that has utility, is unique and nonobvious.

1. To obtain a patent it must be understandable and reproducible by those skilled in the art.
2. The patent must demonstrate that it is functional and not anticipated by prior art.
3. The invention does not need to be practical or economically feasible. Many inventions are never practiced because they are economically infeasible, impractical or do not fulfill a need or provide an improvement or gain.

8.02 What is Innovation?

Innovation: An innovation must be economically practical and producible, fulfill a specific need or create a new opportunity that provides an improvement, gain or profit. It does not have to be an invention.

Innovation is applicable and useful to all types of businesses, organizations or programs.
1. Business innovation introduces useful new ideas and products that meet existing needs or new to the world products that displace existing products or creates demand in new previously undefined

fields or markets.

2. Organizational innovation introduces new methods, procedures and processes that improves and advances the performance and productivity of the business, organization or program.

3. Innovation may range from incremental improvements to revolutionary changes and advances that may displace or disrupt the current status and economic system.

8.03 What Is the Innovation Process?

Innovation Process: is the act or method of creating and identifying a new idea that meets a defined need and converting that idea into a useful product or service that results in an improvement, gain or profit.

1. The process brings together the innovative initiative of all the functions in the organization that work together in parallel toward combining innovative ideas and solutions needed to create the new product or service.

2. It is associated with organizations that lead in the introduction of revolutionary new technologies, products and services that create new to the world systems and markets.

3. It is synonymous with risk taking because the innovators carry the bulk of the investment expense. Imitators assume less risk because they can build on the original innovators knowledge, experience at less expense. However in addition to the original innovative idea, the innovation process encourages the incorporation of

innovative product, process, marketing, etc. ideas in developing the final product which greatly expands the intellectual property protection making it more difficult for imitators.

8.04 Innovation and Innovators

The innovation philosophy and climate created by the visionary 3M leaders in the mid-1900s has proven to be an extraordinarily successful business strategy. Numerous books have been written about 3M Innovation, and companies from around the world have attempted to understand it and emulate it. However, most, if not all, misunderstand 3M innovation. It is commonly perceived as a management and organizational strategy that identifies and implements individual innovation. In other words, innovation is an individual activity.

The book *Steve Jobs*[†] focuses on Jobs as "the" innovator and creator of Apple computers. However, under close examination, he contributed very few of the innovative ideas and technologies that went into Apple computers. The innovations that created Apple came from the organization of innovators that Jobs and his supporters identified and hired. Without them, Jobs could not have created the unique Apple products. Jobs's key contribution was innovating ways of inspiring people and keeping them and the organization focused on the end objective or vision. He understood the "innovation process."

3M Innovation *is* the "innovation process." Essentially all

[†]Walter Isaacson, **Steve Jobs** (Simon & Schuster, November 2011)

innovative products depend upon the integration of multiple innovations from multiple innovators. This requires identifying and assembling supporters, organizations, and teams of innovative people. The key ingredient to 3M Innovation is therefore

> *developing, organizing, encouraging and empowering the men and women throughout the organization to exercise their innovative talent and initiative.*

To create innovative organizations or teams, one must have some understanding of the characteristics of innovators, their type or style of innovation, what drives them to innovate, etc.

8.05 Innovating

Innovating is not just an innovative idea or invention. Innovating or innovation also involves discovering

1. an easier way;
2. a faster way;
3. a time-saving program;
4. a money-saving idea;
5. a new process;
6. a new marketing idea; or
7. a better sales approach.

Dictionaries define innovation as: "something newly

introduced; a new method, custom, device, etc.; a change in the way of doing things."

Obviously, there are many ways of defining innovation. For commercial enterprises, innovation may be defined as

> *new ideas plus action or*
> *implementation, which*
> *results in an improvement,*
> *gain, or profit.*

8.06 Characteristics of Innovators

Everyone is innovative to one degree or another. Who hasn't looked at a situation, a product, or a procedure, and said, "I know a better way of doing that,"? On the other hand, we know that some people are more prolific innovators than others. Therefore, some inherent trait, derived skill, or talent must also be involved.

A talent for innovation may be compared to other talents such as a talent for music. I grew up in a musical family. My father played the guitar, my mother played the piano, and both could sing. One of my sisters plays the piano very well but has never had a piano lesson! She is one of those people who can "play by ear." For myself, I picked up a few of the basic piano skills, but I didn't have the talent that my sister possessed.

However, if my mother had insisted that I take piano lessons and made me practice regularly, I have no doubt that I could have acquired at least some of that skill. (I wish she had!)

The same is true with innovation talent. With encouragement, practice, and the right climate, people can not only make better use of their existing innovative talents but learn to expand them as well.

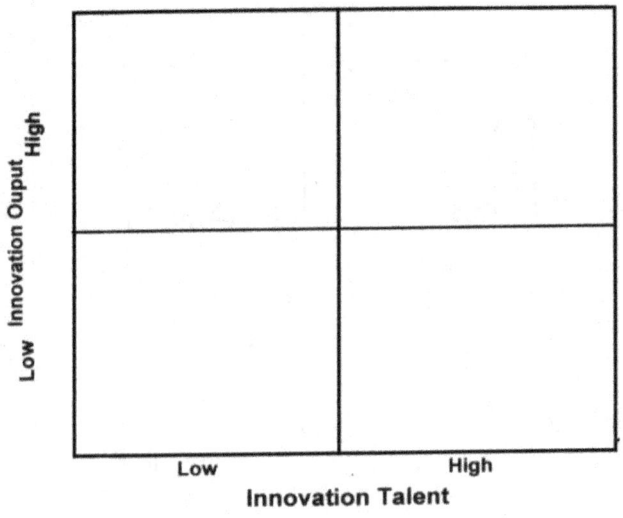

"Dog Chart"

To understand the innovation characteristics of individuals and organizations, it is useful to compare innovative talent to innovative output or productivity. For this comparison, we use a "dog chart." A dog chart has four quadrants with each quadrant defined by the relative level of talent and output. For example, on the horizontal axis we plot low talent to the left and high talent to the right. On the vertical axis we plot low output toward the bottom and high output toward the top.

Individual Innovation:

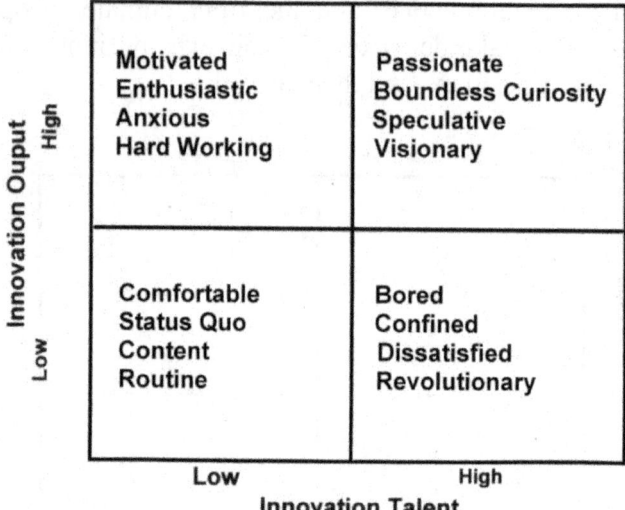

High/High: In the upper-right quadrant, we find people with high talent and high innovative output. People in this quadrant may be characterized as passionate, possessing boundless curiosity, speculative, visionary, etc.

Low/Low: In the lower-left quadrant, we find people who have low talent and low innovative output. People in this quadrant tend to be comfortable with the status quo, be content with performing routine tasks, and ask few questions.

High/Low: In the upper-left quadrant, we find people with low talent but who are very productive. They are generally highly motivated, enthusiastic, anxious to please, and hardworking, particularly with implementation activities.

Low/High: In the lower-right quadrant, we have a rather interesting category. Here are people who have innovative talent, but for one reason or another, they are not exercising it. They are bored, have feelings of being confined, and are usually dissatisfied, prone to revolutionary activities, or likely to leave the organization.

Organization Innovation:

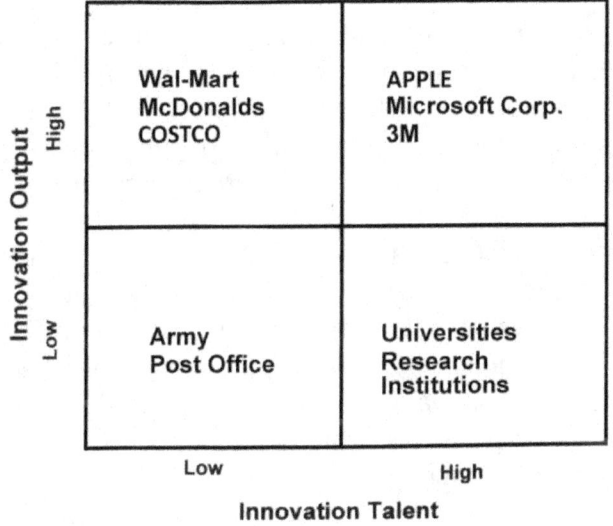

The same chart may also be used to characterize organizations and enterprises.

High/High: In the upper-right quadrant, we find organizations like Apple, Microsoft, Medtronic, and 3M.

Low/Low: In the lower-left, we find organizations like the military, possibly the post office, and other highly routine service organizations.

High/Low: In the upper-left, we find productive service organizations such as McDonalds, Subway, Costco, Macy's, etc.

Low/High: In the lower-right, we have organizations with innovative talent but that are restricted by traditions or management and bound by noninnovative rules, regulations, and policies. This may include universities, research institutions, and routine technical service organizations. The people who stay in the organization tend to become less and less innovative. Others end up leaving to look for more innovative organizations or to establish their own innovative enterprises or businesses.

Innovation initiatives can also take many different forms, some desirable and others not. For example, there are very innovative swindlers, embezzlers, and thieves. Then there is continuous or evolutionary innovation that is brought about by many small, incremental advances in technology or processes. This is useful in sustaining an existing business, but "watch" out!

For example, the Swiss watch industry was recognized as the world leader in timepieces for centuries. They made small, incremental technical advances and improvements to their established product lines. But while they were incrementally innovating, another Swiss innovator developed the first revolutionary electronic watch in the 1960s. Interestingly, the Swiss watch makers chose to remain focused on their established mechanical technology and dismissed the inventor.

However, the inventor didn't go away—he just went to Japan! There he found a willing innovative audience and in a few years the Swiss lost their leadership and it took them decades to recover.

This story also illustrates the need for organizations to develop a dynamic long-term visionary objective that keeps the door open to unanticipated and revolutionary changes in technology and the marketplace.

Also note the role of the "individual" innovator in this story. The individual not only invented the product but also promoted it and played a key role in ensuring the innovation made it into the marketplace. Entrepreneurs are people who do not innovate or invent the new product but who *"manage, organize and assume the risk of a business or enterprise."* So what do we call people who also innovate or invent the new opportunity or product?

One day, while waiting for a plane at the airport, the author Gifford Pinchot sat down next to me and we talked about innovation at 3M. He had been hired by our CEO, Lew Lehr, to write a book about "3M Innovation." We became caught up in attempting to define the type of individual who is not only the entrepreneur but also the inventor or the creator of the product for a new business. I suggested the term "Innoventorpreneur" which is *"one who invents or creates a new product that fulfills a defined need, promotes the new opportunity or product, and manages, organizes, and assumes many risks in establishing a new business based on that product."*

Gifford initially adopted this term and definition but later changed it to "Intrapreneur" which he defined as *"a person in a large corporation empowered to create new products without being constrained by standard procedures."*

He also used this term for the title of his 1985 book[‡] on innovation. (We got so busy talking about innovation that we both missed our planes!)

Driven to Innovate

People innovate for a variety of reasons. As human beings, it is our nature to innovate. We innovate because of our interest in how things work, out of necessity, and for survival. The rate at which we innovate is highly influenced by the current conditions or climate. Given normal conditions, innovative output or productivity is proportional to innovative talent.

This can be illustrated in a graph as a straight line representing innovation productivity going from low output and low talent on the left to high output and high talent on the right.

[‡] Giford Pinchot, *Intrapreneuring: Why You Don't Have to Leave the Corporation to Become an Entrepreneur* (Joanna Cotler Books (August 1985)

Driving Innovation

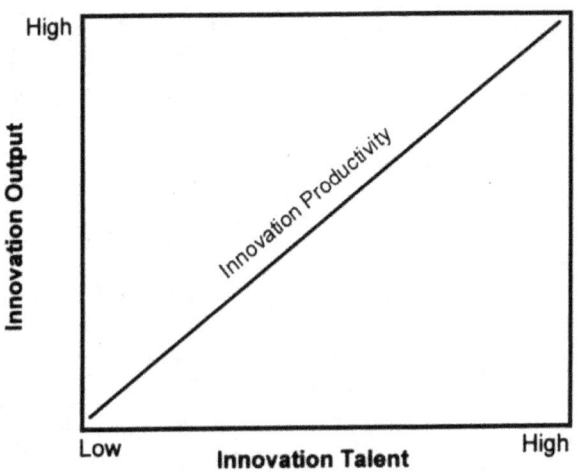

However, we know of organizations that have supportive climates, which causes the productivity line to curve up. We also know of organizations that have repressive climates, which forces the productivity line to curve downward.

Also note that supportive or repressive climates have little effect on the extreme ends of the curve. Those who have little innovative talent are content with the current status regardless of what we do or say. On the other end, we can have people with the insatiable desire to innovate regardless of the climate, and again, there is little we can (or would want to!) do to change this.

Driving Innovation

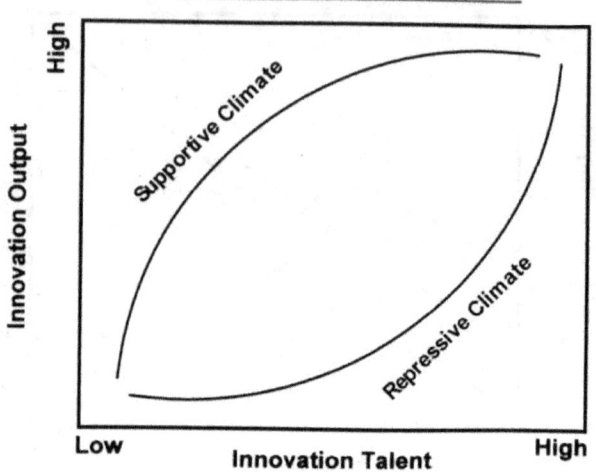

The people we must concern ourselves with are the people in the middle. These people are the most influenced by the climate in which they work. These are the people for which we need to provide the innovative support required to drive the "innovation process."

Incidentally, I chose to use the word "climate" since it relates to the prevailing conditions or attitudes, whereas "environment" relates to the surroundings. Prevailing conditions and attitudes are much more influential in driving innovation than the bricks and mortar.

A supportive climate will provide the innovation for the sustainability, growth, and profitability we want. A repressive climate may provide short-term return and improved profitability, but in the long run, the organization will stifle or die. Nor can innovation be dictated or forced. What happens in this case? The innovative talent is still there, but in the long run, they will shift toward defensive activities and political maneuvering to advance their careers or save themselves.

A defensive shift in innovation is humorously expressed by one of the "idioms" attributed to the character "Dogbert" by Scott Adams:

> ***It is better for your career***
> ***to do nothing than to do***
> ***something and attract attention!***

The innovative talent of the individual is always present. It is only a matter of how it is being applied. Dictatorial management or control that attempts to force innovation will only succeed in suppressing it or channeling it into nonproductive endeavors. It is said that

> ***You cannot kill an idea, but***
> ***you can kill enthusiasm.***

For example, a firm in the Twin Cities manufactured a line of industrial components and devices. Red, one of the managers, convinced his upper management that their technology and products could be redesigned or modified and sold to the residential market. He was given the go-ahead and immediately started to interview applicants. However, before he could hire anyone, he was informed that management had declared a hiring freeze and he wouldn't be allowed to hire anyone from the outside.

He went back to the employment department (i.e., Human Resources) and asked permission to interview employees within the company. However, that was met with resounding "no!" The other department heads weren't about to let their valued employees go.

Undaunted, Red went back to the employment department a second time and discovered that they had compiled a list of employees who had been judged to be the least productive and who had been earmarked for eventual dismissal. He took the list and received permission to interview them for the positions he needed to fill.

Red discovered that most, if not all, of the people on the list were potentially innovative and productive but had been bottled up in departments that restricted or prohibited them from exercising their initiatives and innovative capabilities. After he had filled the positions, he called a meeting and told his new hires why and how they had been selected. They were incensed and astonished to learn that they had been considered to be poor performers. He also told them that it was up to them to exercise their initiatives and innovative skills to build the new business. Within a few years, they created a new residential business that became the leading and most profitable division in the company. Red had created an innovative climate.

In another example, after completing an acquisition of a company, I was informed by the previous owners that we should consider releasing Dick, one of the acquired employees, whom they had judged to be incompetent, lazy, uncooperative, and a misfit. That the owners waited until after the completion of the acquisition to tell me this upset me a great deal. I therefore decided to look into the situation and determine the facts for myself. I immediately arranged a number of interviews with Dick.

The first thing I discovered was that not only he knew about the feelings and opinions of his management but that the other employees knew about it as well, and they were avoiding Dick. He was depressed, withdrawn, and terrified over the possibility of losing his job.

Secondly, I discovered that he was technically very competent and possessed the basic skills in mathematics and optics that we were looking for. When I questioned him about the projects we were working on, he would give a simple answer and end it with "but." I asked him, "What do you mean, 'but'?"

Dick would break out in a sweat and quietly say, "But, I think there is a better solution or a better way," and he would be right!

Every time we met after that, I would ask Dick, "What's new?"—the same question my supervisor Emil Grieshaber had asked me years earlier. At first, Dick struggled, but he always had a new idea, and it wasn't long before he would track me down just to tell me about one of his "new ideas." Dick proceeded to become one of our most prolific innovators and inventors. What a shame it would have been if we had dismissed him as they had recommended.

8.07 Creating an Innovative Climate

Creating an innovative climate requires the commitment and support of everyone in an organization from management on down. Creating the innovative climate requires special skills and techniques. It requires all segments of the organization to be as innovative as they want their organization to be. Regardless of where you end up working or what you do, creating and sustaining a climate for innovation will be your job!

There are three key elements or categories in creating a climate for innovation:

1. **Culture**
2. **Communication**
3. **Style**

In each one of these categories, there are a number of actions or techniques that can be taken or implemented that will encourage and maintain an innovative climate.

I will use the early years of my employment at 3M and the development of the 3M Overhead Projector to illustrate how the above categories influenced and drove innovation.

Culture

Heroes: There were the 3M heroes who demonstrated that it was possible to be successful in promoting your ideas and starting new businesses and, if you did, there would be recognition and reward. There were the innovators who created new technologies and products such as Thermofax by Carl Miller, Scotch tape by Dick Drew, and many more, but also the secretary who solved the sanding belt fraying problem.

Freedom: We not only had the freedom to express our ideas, but it was encouraged, expected, and supported, like at the Friday "show-and-tell" meetings and with the 15 percent rule.

Excitement and Anticipation: There was the excitement and an air of anticipation in what you were doing. Consider the visit by A. J. Bush to see a new development in imaging.

Never Give Up: If management said "no" to an idea or program, we really felt that what it was really saying was, "In its present form, we cannot accept it. Go back and see if you can find a way to make it work." The challenge to develop and design a revolutionary new overhead projector is one example.

Value in Failure: If an idea or project turned out to be unsuccessful, there were no recriminations, and it was recognized that there was value in failure. The Model 26 Check copier turned out to be a failure in the long run, but it led us into a new business of overhead projectors, transparencies, and ultimately "microreplication."

Later in my career, we spent a great deal of time and money developing a unique sound-slide projector. One was able to record a sound or voice message on ordinary 35mm slides. It was a great machine and a great deal of fun to use. However, we had incorrectly read the market. Our vision was faulty. We had responded to the "wants" of the customers and not to their needs.

The problem was that the 35mm slide projection market was changing. People no longer needed a sound-slide projector when video recorders that could display the images on TV screens with sound were becoming available.

Recognizing that we had a white elephant on our hands, we scrapped the project and wrote off several million dollars of investment and inventory. Needless to say, we were all depressed and not sure what our next step was going to be.

Fun: Ray Herzog, our group vice president, got wind of our failure and called a meeting. At the meeting, he expressed his disappointment for the failure of the project. But, he then went on to say that if he had a baseball team where everyone batted 0.300, it would be a good bet that they could win the World Series. He went on to say that if a batter was hitting 0.300, then he must be missing 0.700! In other words, success doesn't come without some misses. He also told us to take advantage of our misses, for by understanding the misses, the batter improves his average. And, by the way, if you are going to bat for 3M, have fun, think big, and try to hit a few home runs while you're at it.

Through it all, we did have fun! We really enjoyed the challenges, the long hours, and working weekends and holidays. We knew that we were doing something important and valuable. Maybe another reason was the celebrations we would have at the end of a successful program involved everyone from management down to technicians.

Communication

Mentoring: Mentoring is a teaching and guiding process and involves one-on-one communication. No one said that my supervisor Emil would be my mentor. He just did it, as did so many others at 3M. It was an assumed responsibility.

Vision: It was Emil who saw to it that we developed a clear vision for what we were doing and that it was shared with everyone.

Ambitious Goals: Ambitious goals were always being set. If I felt the goals were too ambitious or wouldn't work, Emil would say, "I'll bet you a cup of coffee." (I still can't figure out why I would work so hard for a cup of coffee!)

Planning: By setting ambitious goals, we were forced to do a thorough job of planning.

Opening Doors: Emil and Bert were always opening doors for us to help us get the jobs done.

Interfacing with Customers: Opening doors included giving us the opportunity to interface with customers as well as with our own management.

Rewards: Then there were the rewards. There were little rewards like management showing up at 11:00 p.m. with a few treats when we were struggling with the development of a new process or product. There were parties and celebrations after success was achieved. There were also big rewards, on occasion, like unexpectedly being recognized by one of the prestigious corporate recognition programs. Finally, there was the reward of your career growing with your innovations.

Management placed a great deal of emphasis on ensuring that we received credit, recognition, and rewards for our accomplishments. It didn't take credit for the accomplishments of its employees.

Rewards can play very important roles in creating the innovative climate. Researcher Robert Eisenberg and psychologist Teresa Amabile, in their experiments with children as well as adults, found that when rewards were given and expected for each small accomplishment along the way, creativity and innovation declined. However, when the "unanticipated" reward was in recognition of the value of their work and appreciation for what the subjects had accomplished, innovation and creativity were enhanced.

Networking: It is a 3M policy to ensure that networking and communication exists between all employees, including management. 3M established an internal networking program called the "Tech Forum." The objective of the forum is to ensure that the innovations and developments would not only be shared with fellow researchers but with management as well. An annual event is scheduled where technologies and other innovations could be demonstrated and shared throughout the company.

Sending the Right Signals: Communication between employees, supervisors, managers, etc., needs to be clear so that the desired message is heard. For example, a quality control program known as "Crosby Quality Management" promoted the slogan, ***"Do it right the first time."*** On the surface it sounded profound and insightful. The idea was to not rush into a test or program, but to take time and avoid making mistakes.

In practice, it didn't work that way. It assumed that one could anticipate the mistakes and errors ahead of time, which is not possible. In addition, it sent the wrong message to employees. What they heard was "Don't you dare fail!" or "Don't run an experiment until you are sure of success." With that message, failure was not an option. Clearly, that was not the intended response.

It has been said,
> *I'd rather attempt something great and fail, than attempt nothing and succeed!*

Or to put it another way,
> *It's better to do something imperfectly than to do nothing perfectly!*

To correct the mistake, the message was changed to the following:
> *Do it the right <u>way</u> the first time.*

Another example involved a perceived traffic congestion developing around 3M. First, the Minnesota Department of Transportation expressed a concern that the traffic around the 3M center would soon overload the adjacent highways and streets if 3M continued to grow at its current rate. Second, there was an oil embargo underway in 1974 that was creating gas lines and concerns that there were too many cars with single drivers. In response, the 3M engineering department took action. It decided on staggering the starting and ending workday times.

Administrative, marketing, and sales personnel were to start at 7:45 a.m. and leave at 4:30 p.m. Research and engineering personnel were to start at 8:15 a.m. and leave at 5:00 p.m. In addition, a "van pool" program was created. 3M issued a passenger van to an employee who, in turn, would fill it up with fellow employees. Every van, in theory, would eliminate as many as five to seven cars on the road.

There wasn't a traffic problem in the first place. Hours at 3M were already quite flexible, and you could find many people at work long before 8:00 a.m. and long after 5:00 p.m. Traffic was already spread out in the morning and evening hours. Next, when the van pools started, you would find administrative and laboratory people in the same van. So, who was to decide what time the van pool would arrive at work and what time to leave? Unfortunately, many ended up coming to work at 8:15 a.m. and leaving at 4:30 p.m., which severely impacted productivity.

The most undesirable effect of this program was the

signal it sent to employees. What they heard was, "It is more important to stagger working hours, reduce the number of cars on the road, and save gas than it is to innovate, make the extra effort to get a project off the ground, or get a new product out the door on time by putting in some extra hours." By the way, after the program was implemented, it actually "created" a traffic problem. For the first time, large groups of people were now arriving and leaving at the same designated hours, causing traffic congestion.

Style

Sooner or later, as you enter the industrial and commercial world, you will assume coordinative, supervisory, or management responsibilities. "Style" is how employees and the management interface, support, and communicate with one another.

Personal Involvement: It was common for coworkers and those in management to show up to see what you had accomplished or innovated. Frequently, when working late, our management, Bert and Emil, would show up with bags full of doughnuts, White Castle hamburgers, or pizzas.

Be a Servant: Management would then assist us by serving as our technicians.

Eliminate Barriers: On many occasions, management would help overcome or eliminate barriers that stood in our way, like hiring freezes or budget constraints.

Break the Rules: On other occasions, management would let us break the rules, knowing it was the right and productive thing to do.

Trust: We knew that we had the trust of the management team because of the freedom it gave us and because it listened to our ideas.

Faith: Management let us know that it had faith in us by listening to and supporting our ideas.

Credibility: When things weren't going well, management would make sure that we knew the facts and why. For example, when it was recommended that a project be stopped (and that happened on more than one occasion!), we were kept informed and ensured that we were involved in formulating the solution.

Share the Risk: Management knew that we were stretching ourselves both time-wise and technically, but it supported us and shared the risks.

Champions: Coworkers, other employees, and management would volunteer to be our champions by supporting and promoting our efforts throughout the company.

Take Time: Even the corporate president would take time to follow our progress and encourage us.

Receive Credit: Not only did the president follow our progress, the president went out of his or her way to ensure that we received the credit for what we had accomplished.

Empowerment: It was common to empower us to make constructive decisions without requiring endless approvals and reviews.

Attitude: Having a positive and constructive attitude is a key to innovation management.
People with a positive attitude (will-power management)

1. accept new ideas;
2. take risks;
3. have faith in people;
4. have confidence;
5. are willing to share your vision; and
6. tend to respond with "Yes."

People with a negative attitude (won't-power management)

1. resist new ideas;
2. are extremely cautious;
3. have a myopic outlook;
4. focus on operations and controls; and
5. tend to respond to any new idea or proposal with "No!"

9.00 Discussion Topics

9.01 Equipping Your Innovation Toolbox

How do you assemble the skills, knowledge, and resources that you need to drive the innovation process?

9.02 Opportunity Analysis

Is the innovation viable and worth the investment of time and money to bring it to fruition?

9.03 Wants and Needs

What is the difference between "wants" and "needs," and how can it drive innovation?

9.04 Make-a-Little, Sell-a-Little

How do you ensure that the innovation meets the needs of the customers and that the customers will be willing to buy it?

9.05 Risk Assessment, Promoting, and Selling Innovation

What is risk, how is it perceived, why is it important, and can it be managed? How do you promote and sell your innovative ideas and creations?

9.06 Intellectual Property Ownership

How do you protect your innovations and ideas?

NOTES:

9.01 Equipping Your Innovation Toolbox

How do you assemble the skills, knowledge, and resources that you need to drive the innovation process?

Multitasking

No product is as simple as you may think it is. A successful product is almost always not just one but a collection of diverse innovations. Identifying the support innovations needed to develop the primary innovation will speed up the development and success of the project. You don't need to be an expert in all the different technologies and aspects that are needed, but having awareness about them is extremely beneficial. That familiarity will help guide you in assembling the organization of productive innovators needed to support the innovation development process.

Diversity

How do you build and increase your knowledge "about" diverse technologies? Read about them! I strongly recommend making it a regular habit to read books and magazines that will help keep you abreast of recent developments and technologies. I, for one, read (cover to cover) *Scientific American, National Geographic, Smithsonian, Sky and Telescope*, the business section of the newspaper, economic magazines such as *The Economist* (on occasion), etc. Over time, your brain will accumulate a breadth of knowledge that you will draw upon when innovating or when faced with making decisions and organizing your project. In addition, develop hobbies and activities that introduce you to new and diverse techniques and ideas.

Networking

Another important activity is "Networking." Join clubs and other organizations outside of your expertise that will bring you in contact with many diverse people who could possibly possess the expertise or knowledge that you will need down the road.

Discussion

1. List your skills and expertise.
2. List your main interests and favorite activities.
3. What magazines, journals, newspapers, and books have you read?
4. What hobbies do you pursue?
5. What organizations do you belong to?
6. What type or kind of supporting skills might you need to support your personal expertise?
7. Develop a plan to expand your awareness through hobbies, activities, reading, associations, etc.

NOTES:

NOTES:

NOTES:

9.02 Opportunity Analysis

Is an innovation viable and worth the investment of time and money to bring it to fruition?

How can you determine whether or not a new innovative opportunity is potentially viable before significant investments in time and money are made? Formal business and market research studies can be time-consuming and expensive. Obviously, not every idea can be researched in this manner. Further, formal studies are no better than the assumptions they are based upon. Is there a better way?

An early analysis and estimation of the new innovation, even if not precise, not only saves money but can speed its successful development and implementation.

For opportunity analysis, it is helpful to assemble a group of individuals that can focus on the various issues related to the opportunity being studied. Accuracy or precision is not paramount. For example, if a business opportunity is judged to represent a billion-dollar opportunity, it is not harmful if the estimate is off by 50 percent either way. The following are some key considerations to be made in analyzing an opportunity:

1. Clearly define the product.
2. Make a reasonable estimate of the product cost.
3. Identify the market for the product.
4. Define who or what the customers are.
5. Define the customer benefits.
6. Do the customers "want" it or "need" it?

7. How will the customers use the product?
8. Construct a hypothetical business model.
9. Develop a financial model (perform a P&L).
10. Does the opportunity meet or exceed financial goals?

Discussion

1. Use an example of a real-world innovative program or idea and analyze its opportunity. Suggested product programs include the development of the 3M overhead projector and the brightness enhancement film product.
2. Work through the analysis by answering the questions listed above.

NOTES:

NOTES:

NOTES:

9.03 Wants and Needs

What is the difference between "wants" and "needs," and how do they drive innovation?

"Wants" are related to desires whereas "needs" are related to necessities. Generally, "wants" tend to be short-lived and quickly replaced. "Needs" generally relate to the requirements of the customers and may become essential to their operations and ultimate success. There are cases where "wants" and "needs" converge. Given a choice, it is usually desirable to focus on customer needs rather than their stated "wants."

Example: During the development of the overhead projector system, the customers (teachers, presenters, etc.,) "wanted" to make their current tasks easier with minimal changes in what they had been doing. Their "want" was an improvement to their current tools (i.e., the blackboard). However, they "needed" a more efficient presentation and interface system to improve the teaching process and techniques. Once they were exposed to the advantages of the overhead projector system, their "want" also became their "need."

Example: In 1994, Samsung was making a major investment in the production of liquid-crystal displays for electronic devices such as computers, cell phones, and televisions. 3M had developed unique optical films that increased the brightness of the display by factors of two or more. The main advantage the optical films provided was a reduction in the energy needed to power the display. Without the 3M optical films, batteries would have to be two to four times larger, heavier, and expensive. This is a case where the "wants" and the "needs" converged.

The other part of the story is Samsung's "unarticulated need." While touring their optical display assembly operations, we discovered that 75 percent or more of the manufacturing expense was devoted to "cleaning" the optical components going into the display. If any component in the display had a visible defect such as a scratch or dust particle, the entire display would have to be scrapped. To ensure the components were defect-free, numerous time-consuming and expensive cleaning and inspection operations were employed. What they needed was a less expensive and more reliable cleaning system or components that did not need to be cleaned or inspected in the first place.

3M developed a twofold solution to meet their "unarticulated need." First, they were using standard abrasive cleaning materials that inherently left particles and debris on the surface. 3M introduced them to a new class of abrasive material that 3M had developed called "Trizact" that did not contain particulates. This eliminated a major source of contamination and significantly reduced the cleaning expense. Second, 3M implemented clean room conditions in the manufacturing of the optical enhancement films that eliminated defects, contamination, and the need for inspections by Samsung.

Discussion

1. How do you determine the "wants" versus the "needs" of customers?

NOTES:

NOTES:

9.04 Make-a-Little, Sell-a-Little

How do you ensure that the innovation meets the needs of the customers and that the customers will be willing to buy it?

It is natural for innovators to become infatuated with their creations and overlook the real needs of the customers. Having a real customer evaluate and buy the new idea or product at an early stage provides an invaluable test and verification of the design parameters of the new product. However, this must be done with caution. If at all possible, choose a friendly test customer whom you can trust. If necessary, have them sign a confidentiality agreement first. Better yet, make sure you have protected your intellectual property with patents, copyrights, etc., before disclosing the new idea or technology.

Discussion

1. Who should be your first test customer?
2. What qualifications should the test customer have?
3. Ensure a rapid follow-up response to the comments and recommendations of the customer.

NOTES:

NOTES:

9.05 Risk Assessment, Promoting, and Selling Innovation

What is risk, how is it perceived, why is it important, and can it be managed?

"Risk" may be the most overused and misunderstood business term. Risk is commonly viewed as a measure of the probability of failure of an untried new venture or product that could negatively impact the financial well-being and credibility of the organization or the management. Risk is the fear of suffering from the adverse effects of venturing into the new or unknown.

In reality, risk is not the fear or the potential loss of credibility. Risk is a measurement of knowledge. The less knowledge one has, the greater the risk. Conversely, the greater the knowledge one has, the less the risk. Risk is therefore inversely proportional to knowledge.

An innovator who has spent months, if not years, developing a new idea or product will not consider it to be a high risk. However, a person who is exposed to the new idea for the first time will most likely consider it to be very risky, hesitate in investing in it, or even walk away from it. It is essential, therefore, that people with the responsibility to make decisions about the innovation be educated about it at the early stages of development.

Some years ago, I ended up with laboratories in Minnesota, Wisconsin, and California and was puzzled as to where I should locate my office. After some reflection, I decided to locate it near the offices of the 3M business managers and vice presidents.

This ensured closer association with the management and an opportunity to keep them apprised of the technology developments in our laboratories. I made it a practice to take our new innovative samples with me to management and demonstrate them at lunchtime. In most cases, the management became intrigued with and developed an understanding of the new ideas and innovations. By the time an innovation was ready to be reviewed, management already knew about it, had seen it evolve, and frequently became our champion for promoting its development.

Discussion

1. How do you perceive risk?
2. Is there inherent risk?
3. Is risk manageable?
4. Discuss the various types of risk and how it may impact your innovations.
5. What other things can you do to reduce or overcome perceived risk?

NOTES:

NOTES:

NOTES:

9.06 Intellectual Property Ownership

How do you protect your innovations and ideas?

It is essential that new innovations be protected from imitators who are quick to capitalize on your ideas, your investments in time and money, and the value of your innovations. The imitators undercut the value of your ideas. First of all, keep witnessed records of your innovation activities. Keep a patent notebook near you at all times. Second, keep your work as confidential as possible, and if premature disclosure is required, ensure that the appropriate confidentiality agreements have been executed.

If you are creating your own business, be sure to keep at least 51 percent primary ownership of the business and all intellectual property in your name or control at all times.

Discussion

1. Enlist the assistance of a patent agent or attorney to discuss the various methods and procedures for protecting intellectual property.

NOTES:

NOTES:

10.0 Innovator Index

11.0 Subject Index

Technologies

www.ingramcontent.com/pod-product-compliance
Lightning Source LLC
Chambersburg PA
CBHW070246190526
45169CB00001B/318